THE
CHARLES DICKENS
TAROT

Library of Congress Control Number: 2019936083

Cover design by Brenda McCallum

Type set in Dickens McQueen/Minion

ISBN: 978-0-7643-5775-6
Printed in China

Published by Red Feather Mind, Body, Spirit
An imprint of Schiffer Publishing, Ltd.
4880 Lower Valley Road | Atglen, PA 19310
Phone: (610) 593-1777; Fax: (610) 593-2002
E-mail: Info@schifferbooks.com | Web: www.redfeathermbs.com

For our complete selection of fine books on this and related subjects, please visit our website at www.schifferbooks.com. You may also write for a free catalog.

Schiffer Publishing's titles are available at special discounts for bulk purchases for sales promotions or premiums. Special editions, including personalized covers, corporate imprints, and excerpts, can be created in large quantities for special needs. For more information, contact the publisher.

We are always looking for people to write books on new and related subjects. If you have an idea for a book, please contact us at proposals@schifferbooks.com.

Other Schiffer Books that include Charles Dickens references:

A Christmas Tarot: Ghosts of Past, Present, and Future, Dinah Roseberry & Christine "Kesara" Dennett, ISBN 978-0-7643-5568-4

Literary Legends of the British Isles: The Lives & Burial Places of 50 Great Writers, Michael Thomas Barry, ISBN 978-0-7643-4438-1

Chris Leech

THE
CHARLES DICKENS
TAROT

REDFeather™

MIND | BODY | SPIRIT

Printed in China

CONTENTS

Introduction 7

Book the First: Fire 9

Book the Second: Water 23

Book the Third: Air 37

Book the Fourth: Earth 51

Book the Fifth: The Major Arcana 67

Epilogue 112

No Thoroughfare 121

Dickens's Chronological Timeline 124

INTRODUCTION

In *The Charles Dickens Tarot*, the four minor suits have each been reduced to their basic element: **Fire**, **Water**, **Air**, and **Earth**. The standard medieval hierarchy of the court cards has been replaced with the more Victorian **Father**, **Mother**, **Son**, and **Daughter**. The Major Arcana place a special emphasis on the actual life and history of Charles Dickens. One dramatic break from standard Tarot decks is its use of a horizontal orientation, suggesting an open book or vista. Above each card is the card's name, usually indicating its main character. If the card features other characters, the names of the characters appear in the order that they appear on the card, reading left to right. This is followed by a section titled "Shorthand"—a tribute to the shorthand technique Dickens taught himself as a young man, allowing him to record the essentials of a character and situation, as personified by *The Pickwick Papers'* Mr. Jingle. Each Major Arcana card is followed by a section titled "Notes for General Circulation"—a nod to Dickens's *American Notes*.

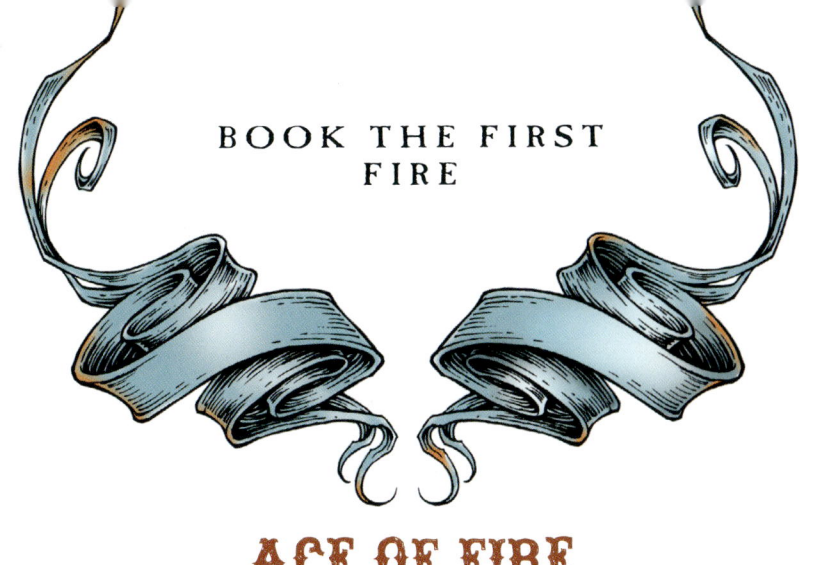

BOOK THE FIRST
FIRE

ACE OF FIRE

ALLUSIONS: The burning of the Houses of Lords and Commons (1834); Satis House; Krook; Mansfield's Law Library; The Sparkler of Albion

SHORTHAND: originality – creativity – virility – primal energy – vigor – conception faculty – inspiration – innovation – invention – pride – overconfidence – wantonness – greed – spark – flash in the pan

OLD MARTIN CHUZZLEWIT

CHARACTERS: Old Martin Chuzzlewit; Mary Graham

BOOK: *Martin Chuzzlewit*

SHORTHAND: willpower – setting a plan into action –
a character of strength and determination – making things happen –
firm rule – all in the service of justice – admirable authority – wealth come by
meretricious means – surprising vitality – true intentions – false starts –
unbridled ambition – rank treachery – deplorable lack of humility – shameful
cheating – overconfident – falters midway – a goal set and achieved –
led, in the end, to a complete revaluation of all goals

THREE OF FIRE

YOUNG MARTIN CHUZZLEWIT

CHARACTER: Young Martin Chuzzlewit

BOOK: *Martin Chuzzlewit*

SHORTHAND: manifest destiny – accomplishment –
an exponential germ – originality fumbles and finds expression –
inspiration well rewarded – perspirational baptism – momentum begets
momentum – the one who realizes stewardship of a calling – dangers implied
– too much, too soon – disillusionment threatens – sickness ensues –
internecine strife – polarizing rancor – spare the rod, spoil the real – dreadful
waste – a goal made a gaol – hard-head – real evolution overlooked

FOUR OF FIRE

BETSEY TROTWOOD

CHARACTERS: Mister Dick; Betsey Trotwood.

BOOK: *David Copperfield*

SHORTHAND: quite self-reliant – fortitude of character – shelter in the proverbial storm – unexpected home – odd family – totally unexpected – fine landing place from which to take off – indubitable agency – very foundation stones of a vocation – proposition: befits a career in the arts – flirts with snobbishness – suffers rigidity – indulges infantilism – posits work is an end in itself – smacks of avoidance – creativity exhausted – enthusiasm grown hidebound – a personal history that ends in prejudice

FIVE OF FIRE

JOHN JASPER

CHARACTER: John Jasper

BOOK: *The Mystery of Edwin Drood*

SHORTHAND: internal strife – where there's smoke there's fire –
head trip – a struggle that seems to have no end – deceit – saying "uncle"
– orchestrated evil – phantasmagoria – unnecessary litigation –
a Pyrrhic victory – an upheaval that can't be avoided – anger – envy –
trickery – losing one's grip – something broken that can't be fixed –
battle so costly it's hardly worth the spoils

THE MERDLES, LAMMLES, & VENEERINGS

CHARACTERS: Hamilton Veneering; Mrs. Merdle; Mr. Merdle, M.P.; Mrs. Lammle; Alfred Lammle; Anastasia Veneering

BOOKS: *Little Dorrit*; *Our Mutual Friend*

SHORTHAND: news – gossip – hearsay – hollow victory – seeming success – too much, too soon – gift horse, foot in mouth: look to it – skillful maneuvering – pantomime – comedy of errors – matchstick men – upstarts – comeuppance – hogwash – high hopes – velvet glove – Greeks bearing gifts

BRADLEY HEADSTONE

CHARACTERS: Lizzie Hexam; Bradley Headstone; Eugene Wrayburn

BOOK: *Our Mutual Friend*

SHORTHAND: such potential – all-consuming – raw animal magnetism – powerful competition – matter over mind – dogged determination – hard headed – hot under the collar – infuriatingly unfair – short fuse – fuel to a fire – nails on a chalkboard – the calling of a bluff – bait and switch – a fall guy

EIGHT OF FIRE

CASBY & PANCKS

CHARACTERS: Christopher Casby; Pancks

BOOK: *Little Dorrit*

SHORTHAND: sudden turnaround – startling outcome –
much movement – crude but effective – the acceleration of facility – striking
while the iron's hot – a certain courage – a persistent wherewithal – a favorable
go-between – great news – cutting to the chase – cooperation – refusing to be
co-opted – possible journeys – impetuous perhaps – rushing headlong

NINE OF FIRE

ABEL MAGWITCH

CHARACTER: Abel Magwitch

BOOK: *David Copperfield*

SHORTHAND: brute strength – stability that cannot
be overthrown – the projection of one's own fear and cowardice – unforeseen
probity – the provision of safety – strength of character – obstinacy –
obdurate – obtuse – suspicion – fortitude – mistreatment – conviction –
foul weather friend – scapegoat

THE CIRCUMLOCUTION OFFICE

CHARACTERS: Tite Barnacle; Clarence Barnacle; Lord Lancaster Stiltstalking; William Barnacle, M.P.; Lord Decimus Tite Barnacle

BOOK: *Little Dorrit*

SHORTHAND: the irresistible object and the immovable force – oppression – suppression – obstinacy – obdurateness – ideas fixed and made unfixable – power for its own sake – lies and deceit – obscurantism – too big to fail – red tape – passing the buck – ineptitude – slow and steady misplaces the race – the center will not hold

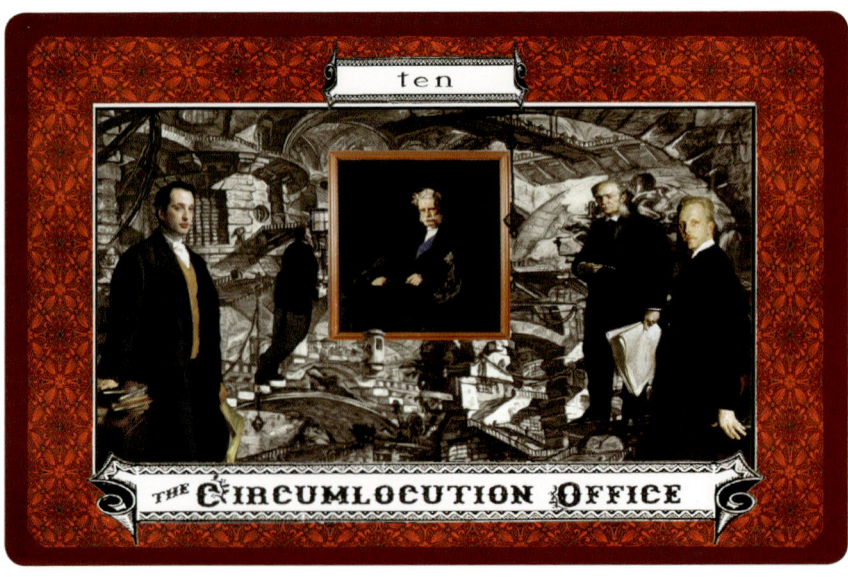

DAUGHTER OF FIRE

DORA SPENLOW

CHARACTERS: Jane Murdstone; Flora Finching; Jip [dog];
Dora Spenlow; Agnes Wickfield

BOOKS: *David Copperfield*; *Little Dorrit*

SHORTHAND: pep – sparkle – enough prettiness to go around
– no stamina – unreasoning and unseasoned – a delightful girl – perhaps
overly cute – apt to break into tears – as light as birdsong in spring – pettish
– undeniably silly – adorable – something of a bore – unsuited to most things
– the unfortunate product of doting – achingly naive – unable to cope –
decisions rash and regrettable – idylls gone idle – pure fancy –
an opening to something else

SON OF FIRE
NICHOLAS NICKLEBY

CHARACTERS: Smike; Nicholas Nickleby

BOOK: *Nicholas Nickleby*

SHORTHAND: quite the lad – a right whippersnapper – alert – active – probably undisciplined – fleet footed – nimble – intolerant but intuitive – unpredictable – even somewhat startling – yet usually seen to be right in retrospect – if self-righteous – drawn to conflict for its own sake – unmistakably enterprising – disobliging – something of a plug nickel – markedly handsome – discursive – perhaps a little facile – in the end, a flash in the pan

MOTHER OF FIRE

MISS HAVISHAM

CHARACTER: Miss Havisham

BOOK: *Great Expectations*

SHORTHAND: by nature, trusting and loving –
strong presence of mind – is herself a force of nature – rarely leaves her
home – is looked up to – has a firm grasp of practical affairs – acts with
authority – sometimes with impunity – she who plays with fire gets burned
– fuming with rage – Hell hath no fury like a woman spurned –
protective of those within her circle – tends to blow smoke

FATHER OF FIRE

RALPH NICKLEBY

CHARACTER: Ralph Nickleby

BOOK: *Nicholas Nickleby*

SHORTHAND: spiteful man – unlikable – would smote 'em
if he had 'em – upright seeming – estimable – may be treacherous – or
lecherous – strong willed – virile – classic creepy uncle – defender of family –
tradition – all ways proper – virtuous according to his own code –
acts the patron – ethical in a narrow, intolerant fashion – will not countenance
effrontery – wears a mask – little more than a name
– a name meaning "counsel" and "wolf"

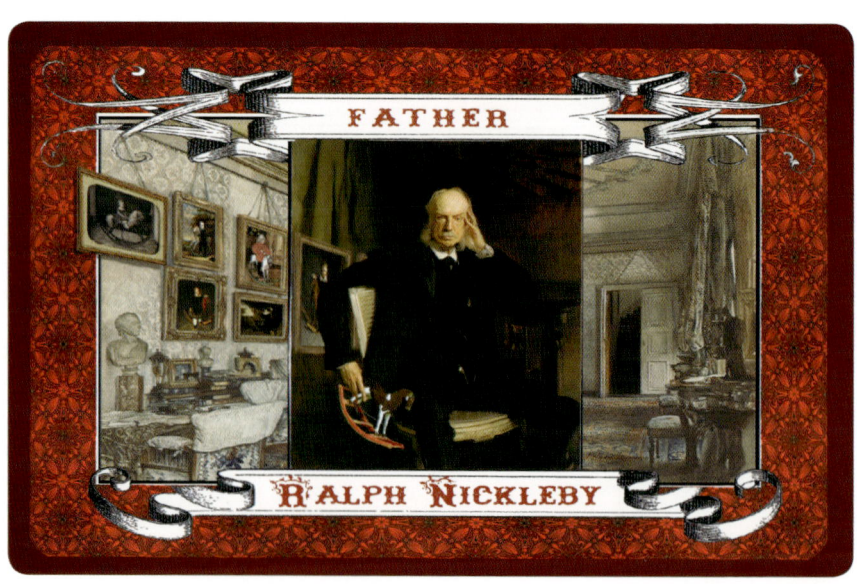

BOOK THE SECOND
WATER

ACE OF WATER

SHORTHAND: feeling – passion – gestation – intuition – nourishment – creation – fertility – despair – fear – sorrow – love – joy – acceptance – family - spirit

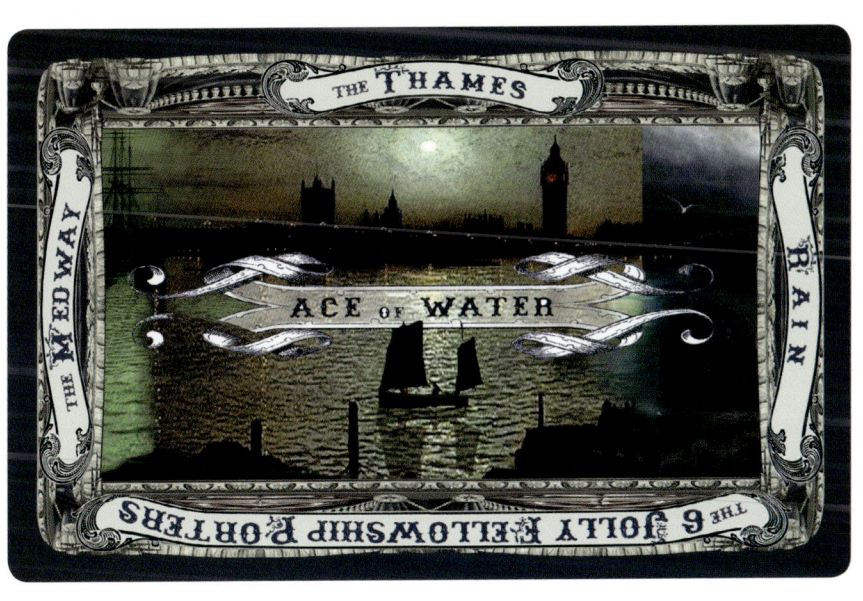

LIZZIE HEXAM & EUGENE WRAYBURN

CHARACTERS: Lizzie Hexam; Eugene Wrayburn

BOOK: *Our Mutual Friend*

SHORTHAND: real passion – emotional affinity – sympathy –
understanding – water seeking its own level – mutuality – mutability –
a reconciliation of opposites – new sensations – jealousies – irresponsibility
– the solution to discord – the end of a rivalry – throwing away an invaluable
gift – hidden intentions – a longing that cannot be denied –
friendship – a treaty – an entreaty – truth and beauty in simplicity –
washing away impurity – a baptism of love

THE CRUMMLES STROLLING PLAYERS

CHARACTERS: Master Crummles; Vincent Crummles;
Mr. Curdles; Mrs. Crummles; Mr. Snevellici; Miss Bravassa;
Percy Crummles; Thomas Lenville; Miss Snevellici

BOOK: *Nicholas Nickleby*

SHORTHAND: what fun – harmony – solicitation –
love's labors won – healing ills through happiness – manna from heaven –
meaningless diversion – somewhat indulgent – exploitation of emotion –
amusement – gift of the muses – the value of an enterprise conceived in love
– heartfelt but poorly staged – sociability – shared interests –
some anger at having to share the limelight

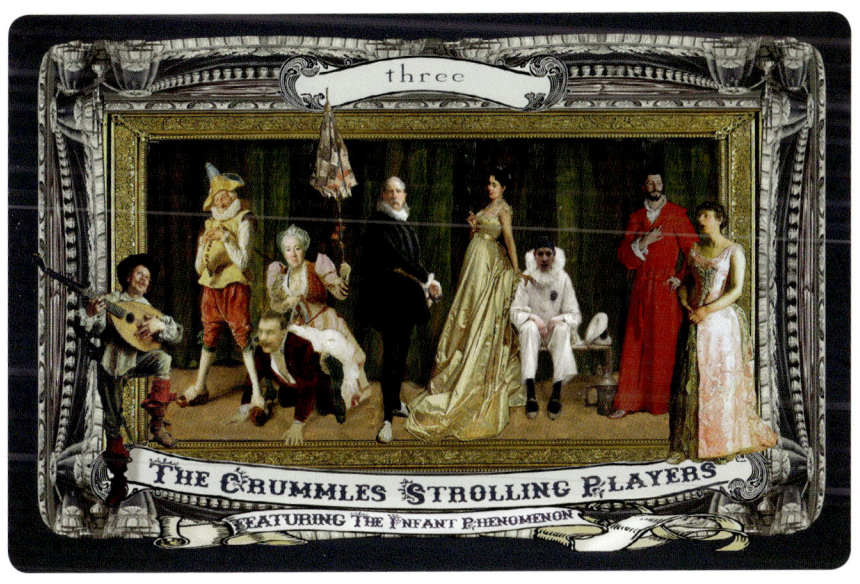

FOUR OF WATER

JAMES STEERFORTH

CHARACTERS: Little Em'ly; James Steerforth

BOOK: *David Copperfield*

SHORTHAND: dissipated past – such promise –
a dissatisfaction the things of this world cannot assuage – high handed
– base apathy – too handsome – disabuse – excesses of all kinds – no
discipline – no bearing – false idols – idle class – eidolon – self-seeking
ingrate – in short: visionary insight

FIVE OF WATER

ROSA DARTLE

CHARACTER: Rosa Dartle

BOOK: *David Copperfield*

SHORTHAND: happiness gone – strings attached – remorse – hardened heart – sharp edges – cutting – deep grief – cowed but not cowardly – expression and impotence – frame of mind – disfiguring – on high, white; down here, black – Cupid and Psyche – possible spearhead of art – horrible harping on

AARON RIAH AND JENNY WREN

CHARACTERS: Aaron Riah; Jenny Wren

BOOK: *Our Mutual Friend*

SHORTHAND: hard-won happiness – harmony – well-being – strange bedfellows – prejudice overcome – a unique niche – finally reaping what was sewn – nostalgia – infantilization – hiding away from the world – new clothes from old cloth – working through a difficult past in the here and now to achieve a pleasant future – a dream come true

LITTLE NELL'S GRANDFATHER

CHARACTER: Little Nell's Grandfather

BOOK: *The Old Curiosity Shop*

SHORTHAND: a game of chance – a bet or a bluff – a decision
– the road to Nell is paved with good intentions – bewitched – false hopes –
confusion – hallucinations – the fabulous – ways of seeing – completely
mystified – deception – curiosity – motley – discursive – derangement – lack
of discipline – apologue – poor choices – abreaction – all or nothing

STEPHEN BLACKPOOL

CHARACTER: Stephen Blackpool

BOOK: *Hard Times*

SHORTHAND: nowhere else to go – a change of heart – *force majeure* – burning bridges – caught between two stools – rejection of established relationships – going it alone – pursuing some impossible ideal – something deeper attained, if at great peril – a disillusion with community – impetuous – impetus – impotence – eschewal – unsure footing – hightailing it – a new and possibly imposed perspective

NINE OF WATER

JOHN WEMMICK

CHARACTERS: The Aged Parent; John Wemmick; Miss Skiffins

BOOK: *Great Expectations*

SHORTHAND: well-being – safe and sound – self-satisfied –
self-contained – emotional quid pro quo – I'm all right, Jack – portable probity
– *comme il faut* – possible sentimentality – indulgences – dissociation –
protectionism on a personal scale – overlooking the faults in others –
leads to an abuse of hospitality

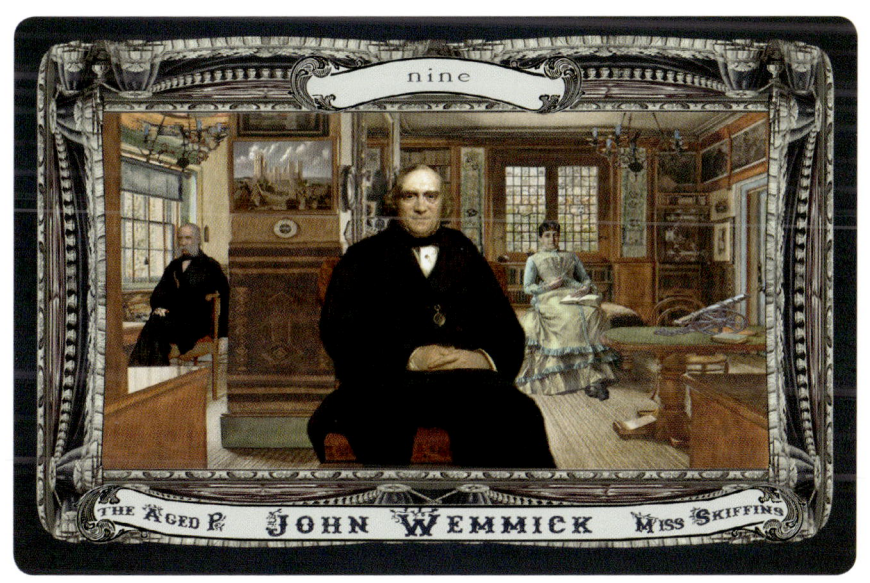

YARMOUTH

CHARACTERS: David Copperfield; Little Em'ly; Ham Peggotty; Daniel Peggotty

BOOK: *David Copperfield*

SHORTHAND: peace – security – a sense of family – acceptance – salad days – coziness – bucolic surroundings – antisocial actions – feeling sorry for oneself – nostalgia – exploitation of the goodwill of others – betrayal of friends – disruption of familial order – taboo attractions – wistfulness – psychological displacement

DAUGHTER OF WATER

ESTHER SUMMERSON

CHARACTERS: Esther Summerson; Allan Woodcourt

BOOK: *Bleak House*

SHORTHAND: perspicacious – cautious but frank – sincere to a fault – proverbial provocation to growth – deep capacity for understanding – unexpected insight from an overlooked quarter – awkwardly painstaking – infuriating discretion – liable to self-deception – smells of overpruning – possible martyr complex – yet uncanny of foresight – profound appreciation of beauty – in the end, lacking the temperament to be an artist

DAVID COPPERFIELD

CHARACTER: David Copperfield

BOOK: *David Copperfield*

SHORTHAND: amiable boy – enthusiasm in spades – sensitive – open hearted – artistic soul – restless spirit – a fair and fine figure – downright lovable – may be something he's not – something of a dissembler – cute as the dickens – makes his own opportunities – the hero of his own life – learns from suffering – heartfelt focus on family – weakness for driveling – shows a marked inability to discern where truth ends and falseness begins

MOTHER OF WATER

CLARA PEGGOTTY

CHARACTERS: Clara Peggotty; Clara Copperfield

BOOK: *David Copperfield*

SHORTHAND: affectionate – blushing – a girl herself – romantic in outlook – dutiful, if not exactly beautiful – capable of unconditional love – instincts that can be relied on – sentimental – a wonderful companion in grief – stronger than she looks – easily influenced by events and people – exudes happiness – may be crushed by malevolent forces – can be all things, if not to all men, at least to all little boys

FATHER OF WATER FIRE

JOE GARGERY

CHARACTERS: Georgiana Mary Pirrip; Joe Gargery; Biddy

BOOK: *Great Expectations*

SHORTHAND: the proverbial gentle giant –
warm – patient – loved if not always respected – easy to take for
granted – forges lasting relationships – shy – works humbly behind
the scenes –all heart – forgiving – possibly too giving –
paralyzed by his own goodness

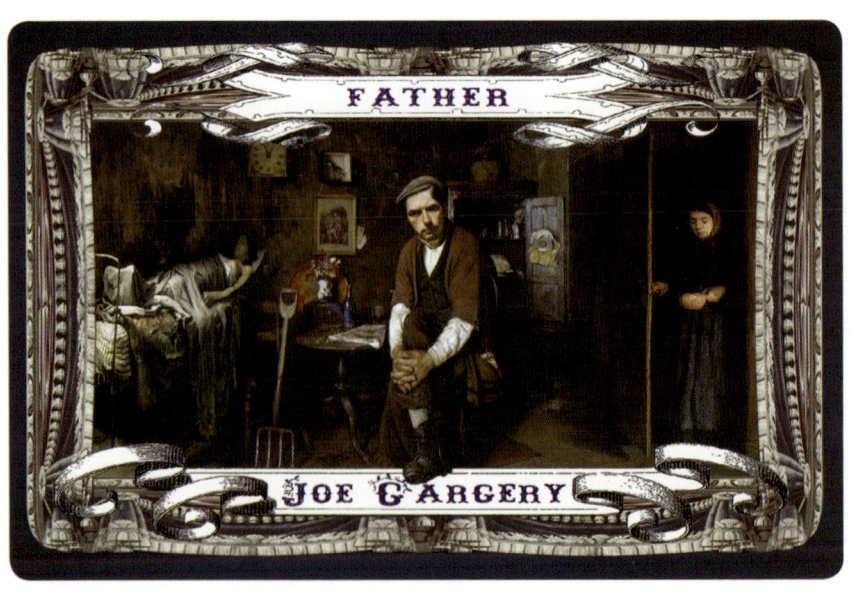

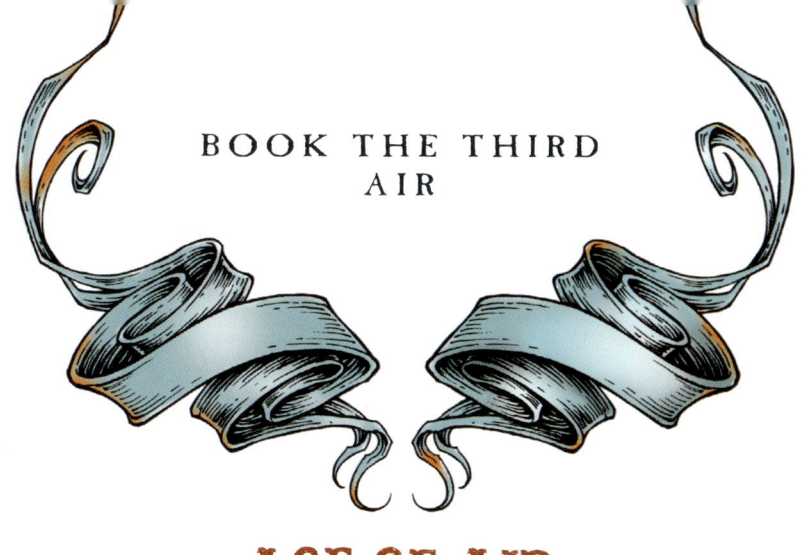

BOOK THE THIRD
AIR

ACE OF AIR

SHORTHAND: thought – victory – justice – rationale – authority – discernment – judgment – authority – change – analysis – destruction – restriction – idealism – obsession – will

MADAME THÉRÈSE DEFARGE

BOOK: *A Tale of Two Cities*

SHORTHAND: égalité – the conflict of opposing forces –
an eye for an eye – hard choices – severity – tough love – truth or truce –
weighed in the balance and found wanting – discord for its own sake –
dudgeon – rage – righteous indignation – abuse of power – vigilante justice
– amputation – polemics – a critical point – which side are you on? –
fraternité leaves out femmes – live by the sword, die by the sword –
sacrificial lamb – heads or tales? – *vive la différence*

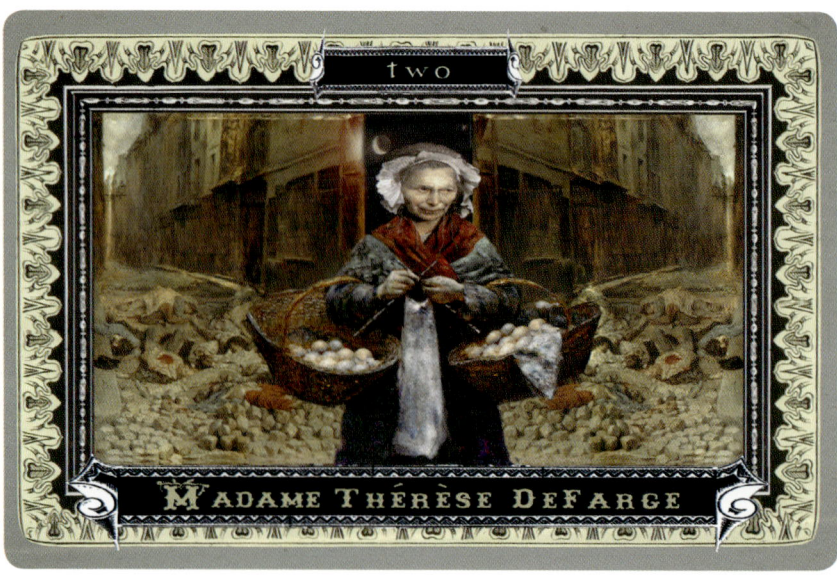

THREE OF AIR

MRS. SARAH GAMP

CHARACTER: Sarah Gamp

BOOK: *Martin Chuzzlewit*

SHORTHAND: death of sentimentality – lies – deceits –
falsehoods revealed – in a pickle – gin fizz – self-deluded – to harass with
Harris – physical disorder – mental distress – cutting away the fat –
under the weather – loss of patience – a call for reform – gasbag –
midwife crisis – good night, nurse!

WILLIAM DORRIT

CHARACTER: William Dorrit

BOOK: *Little Dorrit*

SHORTHAND: much dignity – probably too much –
balm through troubled times – venerable old-timer – stoic to a fault –
austere indeed – reconciliation of sorts – recuperating from battles lost
– making the best of a bad situation – mind over matter – sad sanctuary –
mere hospitalization – some bending of the knee – seeks assistance from
outside sources – what do you know? a windfall! – cowardly reluctance to
countenance reality – compensating delusions of grandeur – debts paid
– coming to terms with one's past – at last, surrender

THOMAS GRADGRIND

CHARACTER: Thomas Gradgrind

BOOK: *Hard Times*

SHORTHAND: pedantic twit – denier of everything supple and human – the utter impracticality of utter practicality – defeat – loss – dishonor – all must be accepted before any thought of future success – insufferable stubbornness – chickens that come home to roost – pride swallowed – order as a way to disguise disorder – double-dealing – a pedagogue – hoist by his own smoke and mirrors

THE MANNETTES & MISS PROSS

CHARACTERS: Dr. Alexandre Manette; Lucie Darnay *the younger*;
Lucie Darnay *the elder*; Miss Pross

BOOK: *A Tale of Two Cities*

SHORTHAND: action: solution to problems? –
an eye for an eye, a shoe for a shoe – such is an obstacle temporarily
overcome – a partial success – a question, to be sure: just what is progress?
– rescue? – banishment? – the past cannot be escaped – the future impossible
to elude – the terrible tenterhooks of the present – but a momentary reprieve
– yet heeding the call for continuing effort – doctor heels thyself –
supposition: that difficulties fled without resolution will only resurface –
the shoe, in the end, on the other foot—if it ever falls

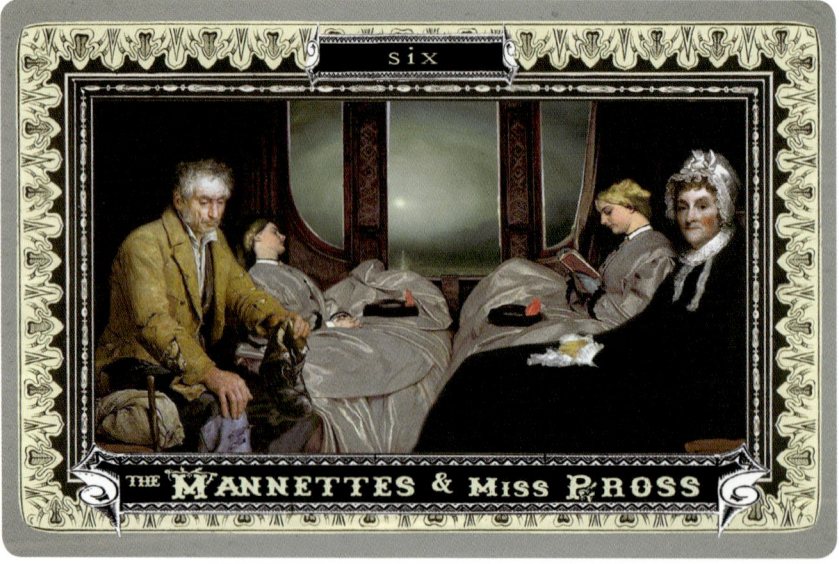

SEVEN OF AIR

URIAH HEEP

CHARACTERS: Mr. Wakefield; Uriah Heep; Mrs. Heep

BOOK: *David Copperfield*

SHORTHAND: unctuous – bereft of eyebrows –
the proverbial snake in the grass – aggrandizing self-abasement –
cockney rhyming slang for creep – backstabber – blind ambition – deceitful
– a real cautionary tale – cunning employed – humiliation avoided – the
enemy's weaknesses used to great advantage – attempted entrapment –
yet courage – even audacity – vile manipulation

EIGHT OF AIR

NANCY

CHARACTER: Nancy

BOOK: *Oliver Twist*

SHORTHAND: bondage – isolation enforced – severe difficulties – outward physical force vs. internal strength of will – resolute apperception – indoctrination to the contrary – demoralization systematic – chance alignment – menace overcome – dastardly cunning – evil vanquished from within – a sacrifice here, the result: a salvation over there – assumption of villainy itself be villainous – the cycle of adversity, broken – wondrous Truth, revealed – for better and/or for worse – rather forfeit, exacting cost – grasping at opportunity – ideas brooded and hatched – renunciations effaced – greater good – deep despair – certain fear – loyalties torn asunder – betrayal – furtiveness – self denied – possible martyrdom – altruism in all likelihood – self-righteousness now and again – violent submission – a life, in short, owed to another's sufferance

LADY HONORIA DEDLOCK

CHARCTER: Lady Honoria Dedlock

BOOK: *Bleak House*

SHORTHAND: deception – gilded shame – internalized guilt –
fine cruelty – circuitous punishment – naturally scandal – uncontrollable
passion – some malice – some misery – slander – self-denial and self-
abasement – all combated with resignation – obedience – calculated inaction
– paralysis resulting – an impossible running away – crestfallen
comeuppance – all done in dumb show – queer sense of imposing
– the calling card of martyrs – sacrificial lamb on the lam – sheepishness –
private anguish frozen – attention diverted – core responsibility snowed
under – root causes whitewashed – slate wiped clean

BILL SIKES

CHARACTER: Bill Sikes

BOOK: *Oliver Twist*

SHORTHAND: terrible man – terrible dog – thank god
they're dead, even though suffering continues – a fine end – those who
live by the sword, die by the sword – the worst may be past –
out of *sikes*, out of mind

DAUGHTER OF AIR

ESTELLA

CHARACTER: Estella

BOOK: *Great Expectations*

SHORTHAND: cutting – an air of superiority –
an apt pupil – sharp tongued – remote – shining – singular –
unattainable – devious and vindictive – star crossed – seeks out hidden
weaknesses – cold as ice – hard as a diamond – professes friendship –
toys, but is herself being toyed – too clever by half – incapable of love –
unlovable – in the end, small and pitiable

SON OF AIR

JONAS CHUZZLEWIT

CHARACTERS: Montague Tigg; Jonas Chuzzlewit; Anthony Chuzzlewit

BOOK: *Martin Chuzzlewit*

SHORTHAND: a man who rises to a challenge – a crafty devil – stronger than we thought, but maybe not as strong as he thought – not afraid of killing, but afraid of being killed – heedless of warnings – plunges headlong into headstrong – cruel – unusual – believes little fish simply get eaten by big fish – tends to start things he can't finish

MOTHER OF AIR

MRS. CLENNAM

CHARACTER: Mrs. Clennam

BOOK: *Little Dorrit*

SHORTHAND: severe, to be sure – attentive to detail –
biblical bitterness – psychosomatic condition – holier than thou – poison
penance – love leveraged and withheld – factitious of reasoning – rigidity,
brittle – punctilio – alert to motive – high of opinion, high of hand –
formidable adversary – righteousness employed as smokescreen – strange
inability to forget – genuine desire for atonement –
a deathbed repentance at last

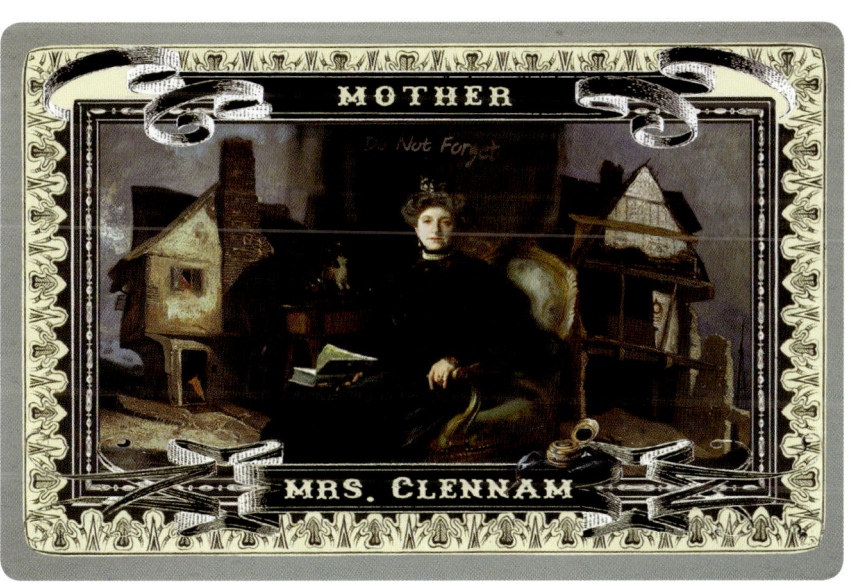

FATHER OF AIR

DANIEL QUILP

CHARACTER: Daniel Quilp

BOOK: *The Old Curiosity Shop*

SHORTHAND: quite an original turn of mind – relishes authority – resourceful – astute – relentless in pursuit of his quarry – contrived – severe – inconsistent of plan – an inveterate game player – too big for his britches – a Napoleon complex – fan of modernity – a serviceable villain – deliberately cruel – calculating – sadistic – impersonal – capable of the utmost evil – libidinous

BOOK THE FOURTH
EARTH

ACE OF EARTH

SHORTHAND: physical beauty – sensuousness – sensation – material comfort – security – terra firma – stoicism – steadfastness – avarice – materialism – complacence – habit – stoicism – spirit attained through abundance

DICK SWIVELLER

CHARACTERS: Sampson Brass; The Marchioness; Dick Swiveller; Sally Brass

BOOK: *The Old Curiosity Shop*

SHORTHAND: something afoot – the fluctuations of fortune – overheard news – miscommunications – journeys of discovery – double dealings – double duty – brass tacks – lightheartedness – newfound pleasure – redoubled wisdom – good riddance to bad riddles – inconsistencies – injustices unearthed – sibling rivalry – not getting unhinged – turning to good account – unforeseen developments – juggling matters – the art of misdirection – unmasking the two faced – sortilege

SETH PECKSNIFF

CHARACTERS: Mercy "Merry" Pecksniff; Seth Pecksniff; Charity "Cherry" Pecksniff

BOOK: *Martin Chuzzlewit*

SHORTHAND: commercial business – a bold venture – building prosperity – hope springs infernal – be careful what you wish for – schemes and designs – sketchy – castles built on sand – false flattery – conceit that prevents one from establishing anything worthwhile – artificiality – unable to learn from criticism – wanting something from nothing

FOUR OF EARTH

JOSIAH BOUNDERBY

CHARACTERS: Tom Gradgrind; Josiah Bounderby; Louisa Gradgrind

BOOK: *Hard Times*

SHORTHAND: covetous cad – stable materially – mentally stale – monetary problems are over – deeper problems just beginning – the establishment of a financial empire – the establishment of a commercial empire – a human disconnect – centralization of power – possessions used to bolster one's ego – holding so tightly to the letter of the law it chokes to death the spirit – in the end: counterfeit and forged

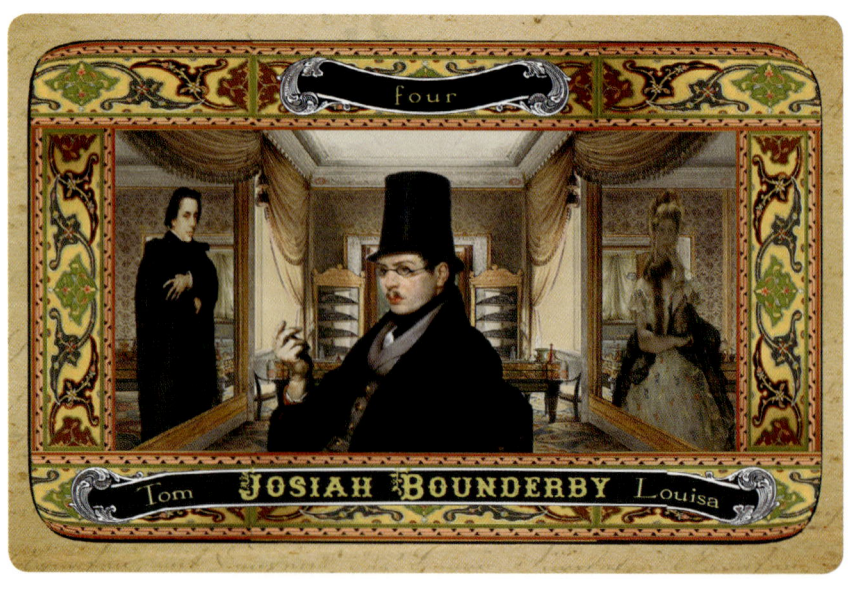

BOB CRATCHIT AND TINY TIM

CHARACTER: Bob Cratchit; Tiny Tim

BOOK: *A Christmas Carol*

SHORTHAND: poverty – destitution – material worries – overworked and underpaid – no financial security, but love and family – generosity of spirit – charitable of heart – possible adversity afoot – important bonds formed under trying circumstances – unexpected avenues may yet open – selfish interests threaten the greater good – making the best of what you have – do not despair

JOHN JARNDYCE

CHARACTERS: Mrs. Jellyby; a Jellyby child; Emma Neckett;
Mrs. Pardiggle [portrait]; John Jarndyce; Charlotte "Charley" Neckett; Gridley,
a.k.a. the Man From Shropshire; Harold Skimpole

BOOK: *Bleak House*

SHORTHAND: card of the philanthropist – power used to raise –
position used to place others – heartfelt empathy – well-met gratitude – doing
good and do-gooding – the rewards of wardship – patronage – very sound
advice – veritable room at the inn – riches redistributed – care of community
– strength in numbers – magnanimous display – lurking paternalism – motives
self-serving – wretched charity begins at home – goodwill abused –
"poor me" – no of self-discipline – growing profligacy – final dissipation

SEVEN OF AIR

LITTLE PAUL DOMBEY

CHARACTERS: Dr. Blimber; Paul Dombey Junior; P. Toots

BOOK: *Dombey & Son*

SHORTHAND: wishful thinking – possible material success –
all your eggs in one basket – efforts in the past may lead to prosperity in the
future – investment – self-induced worry – square pegs in round holes –
good money after bad – warning that loss is imminent – make hay while the
sun shines – securing the fruit of one's labor at emotional and spiritual cost
– the misappreciation of fortune

EIGHT OF EARTH

KIT NUBBLES

CHARACTER: Kit Nubbles

BOOK: *The Old Curiosity Shop*

SHORTHAND: nurturing child – steadfast – exceptional pluck – such perseverance is no gamble – skills surely need developing – pleasure in the little things – honesty prevails – mischief in business affairs – garlands for the diligent – gainful employment for the able – rumors of misconduct – misunderstandings ironed out – short-term loss but long-term gain – the constant threat of diversions – it all comes out in the wash

BELLA WILFER

CHARACTERS: Bella Wilfer; Reginald "Rumty" Wilfer

BOOK: *Our Mutual Friend*

SHORTHAND: much comfort – belongings – sound of body – clear of sight – verve and wisdom – material success – prosperity all around – hints of devious means – perhaps rapture – alchemy – clipping of wings – warming – charming – domesticated dreams

BOFFIN'S BOWER ·

CHARACTERS: Nicodemus "Noddy" Boffin; Silas Wegg;
Vincent Venus; Henrietta Boffin

BOOK: *Our Mutual Friend*

SHORTHAND: great inheritance – odd family – dirty trade
– the stone the mason threw away – accumulated income – material wealth
– jolly good fortune – unquestionable will – gratis help – bowery dowry –
what's the word? – the world too much with us – concerns of legitimacy
– the culmination – the value of value – the matter, sifted

DAUGHTER OF EARTH

FLORENCE DOMBEY

CHARACTERS: Walter Gay; Florence Dombey;
Captain Edward Cuttle

BOOK: *Dombey & Son*

SHORTHAND: conscientious – responsible – diligent –
dutiful – perhaps lacking humor – sound business sense – overlooked
treasure – value misplaced – earnest to a fault – resourceful –
honorable – good head on her shoulders – noble by nature – hard done by –
proves her worth – father issues – self-sacrificing – willful –
will, with the slightest attention, flourish

JOHN HARMON

CHARACTER: John Harmon

BOOK: *Our Mutual Friend*

SHORTHAND: odd young man – morally upright –
defender of what's true – yet hits himself something of a false note –
practical rather than abstract – good with numbers – hands-on –
struggles with established authority and judging for himself – perhaps overly
cautious – doesn't give much away – solid but stolid – slow to action – a little
wet behind the ears – so patient he might be ill – willing to work pro bono

MOTHER OF EARTH

AMY DORRIT

CHARACTER: Amy Dorrit

BOOK: *Little Dorrit*

SHORTHAND: down to earth – sensible – sensitive – wise – compassionate – adorable – giving – forgiving – understands the true value of things – not unduly intelligent – loyal – perhaps narrow of outlook – a life circumscribed by the material – able to rise above almost any matter – when one door opens, another closes – suspicious of what she does not understand – sometimes a little arch – able to bridge people's differences

PAUL DOMBEY

CHARACTERS: Florence Gay; Paul Dombey; Paul Gay

BOOK: *Dombey & Son*

SHORTHAND: cautious – methodical – perhaps mechanical – old-fashioned – stuck in the past – dull – materialistic – capable of deep thought and feeling, only he doesn't always engage – slow to give affection – unable to adapt to change – committed to outmoded ways – hides his weakness in grandeur – insular – afraid of the transitory – impervious to beauty – commands loyalty – fears his own feelings and responds by being implacable – proof positive change must come from within – acceptance and bounty will follow

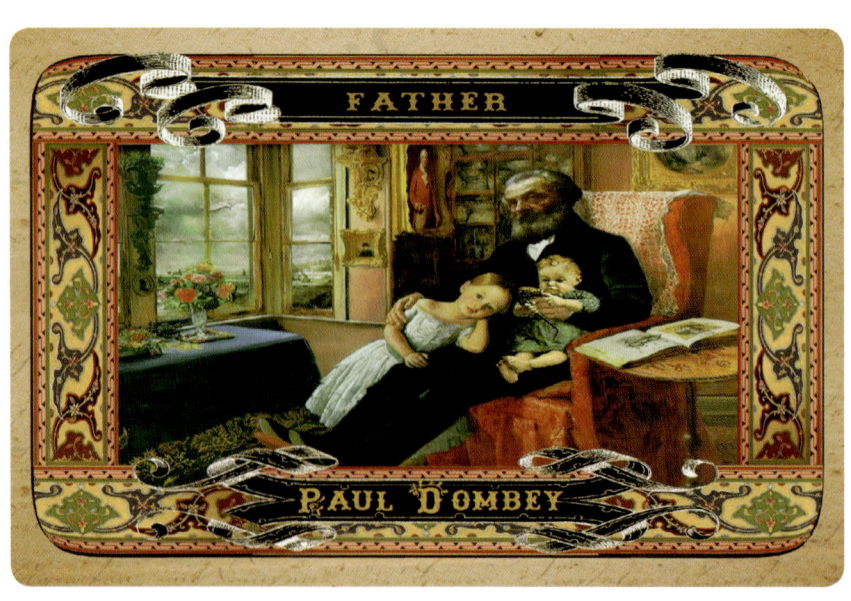

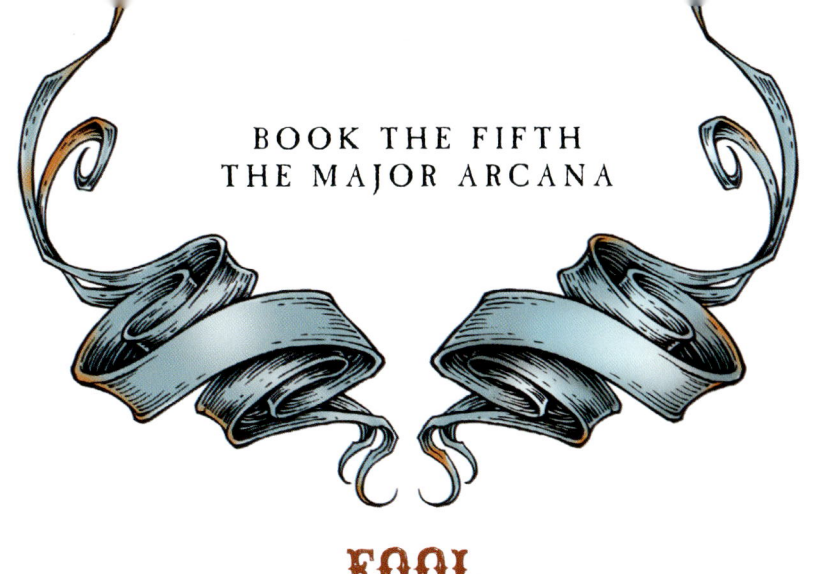

BOOK THE FIFTH
THE MAJOR ARCANA

FOOL

CHARACTERS: Samuel Pickwick; Samuel Weller

BOOK: *The Pickwick Papers*

NOTES FOR GENERAL CIRCULATION:

- The unnumbered card of the Tarot's Major Arcana signifies the fundamental condition in which man finds himself in the world. We may assume Mr. Pickwick carries in his valise the nineteenth-century symbolic equivalents of the elements Earth, Air, Water, and Fire—or perhaps his bag is empty so he can fill it with the aforesaid elementary samples he finds along his way. It may be said that Pickwick looks a little self-pleased—or able to break the fourth wall and smile directly at the reader.

- The traditional dog figure, symbolizing man's animal nature and the animal's sorrow at seeing his companion foolishly striving headlong toward the unnatural, is here replaced by his loyal page, Samuel Weller. Pickwick's journey is indefinite and may indeed require Weller's services as a bootblack. That the polish he uses for the job is Warren's Blacking seems unquestionable.

- *Pickwick*'s almost insistent lack of structure is the Fool's most unifying motif. The card's lack of number represents its lack of name, the sound a child makes, a blank left for the reader himself to fill in.

- This card's appearance in a formal pattern usually means two things:

    1. The reader needs to have a look at what it is they have in their hands, and
    2. The reader has set out on a venture, which needs to be seen as such and demands the reader strives on some level to understand.

- It is not linked with any planetary influences; rather, it is the empty space between planets. The Fool indicates unexpected influences, coincidence, luck, Providence, and the unplanned.

- The Fool may suggest the divine, the infinite wellspring of creativity, or the birth of an exceptionally creative person. It may also indicate the loss of innocence, recklessness, and the Fall of Man, which results in the rational but senseless bondage of the Soul.

I. THE MAGICIAN CHARLES DICKENS

CHARACTERS: Arthur Clennam; Daniel Doyce

ROMAN À CLEF: Charles Huffam Dickens, a.k.a. Boz

BOOKS: *Little Dorrit*; *Sketches by Boz*

NOTES FOR GENERAL CIRCULATION:

- **The Magician** represents the man as he is: the enchanter, the marvel, magic wand in hand.
- **The Magician** is an incredibly rich representation of humanity's capability, the level of consciousness available to mankind.
- **The Magician** looks directly at his audience, the reader. He looks on his audience for recognition and inspiration, and his audience looks to him for

the same. He may have little personality of his own as yet, but his energy and charm more than make up for it.

- His control over his prolific creativity is signified in the borders of the Minor Arcana, which frame him. There may be some suggestion, however, that they are being used here by **The Magician** merely as decoration.

- The white quill Boz holds may indicate the divine nature of his endeavor, a feather from the peace dove or the Paraclete. The black ink and its well may suggest darker aspects circulating beneath the surface. The table Boz poses before, bisecting the card and concealing **The Magician**'s lower half, signifies the division between heaven and Earth.

- **The Magician** is traditionally associated with Gemini, ruled by the planet Mercury. Mercury the god is a trickster, a messenger of the gods, whose name is derived from *merchant* and indicates commerce. The division of **The Magician** into three characters suggests Mercury's triadic glyph.

- **The Magician**'s appearance in a formal pattern may indicate change is needed—of career or of attitude. The central cross and somewhat fylfot aspect of the card suggests disparate aspects need to be pulled together or that details need to be focused on. If the reader is female, **The Magician's** need for an audience's approval may imply a male who will turn out to be not entirely satisfactory.

- **The Magician** represents the mercurial impulse toward speech, the written word, or acting. It indicates the ability to take risks, an alert intelligence, and a persuasive eloquence. It may also indicate cowardice, hubris, and charlatanism—especially as it relates to man's blindness to his own spiritual condition. Because **The Magician** is affiliated with Gemini, the dualism or divided nature of which is essential to the card's understanding—a point iterated in the split inspirational and facilitating aspects of Doyce and Clennam.

II. THE HIGH PRIESTESS
ELLEN TERNAN

CHARACTERS: Lucie Manette; Estella; Bella Wilfer; Helena Landless

ROMAN À CLEF: Ellen "Nelly" Lawless Ternan

NOTES FOR GENERAL CIRCULATION:

- The second card of the Major Arcana represents the passive side of humanity. The first card is active, male, outward moving; the second card is female, reflective, inward revealing. She signifies the conditions necessary for the development of the spiritual.

- **Blue dominates**—the color of sensitive passivity. The three frames create a strong triadic force. They indicate the rigid boundaries imposed by society; here, the Victorian era's behavioral dictates. The loose-flowing sheets enveloping a woman's naked body indicate the nature and reality that society would outlaw and conceal. The book that **The High Priestess** holds may

signify esoteric knowledge; it may symbolize the cherished works of a great author; it may be a book as yet unwritten. The ring she holds is one she cannot wear. The key is a skeleton key and may fit just about any door. The card's usual double wimple is replaced by the unfurling sheets of a courtesan, or are they wings? Or a settling shroud? Whatever they may be, they intimate cold receptivity.

- **The High Priestess** would be looking directly out at the reader if she could. **The Magician** of the previous card, with his back to her, is doing what he can to look the other way. **The Empress**, meantime, is oblivious.

- In a formal pattern, **The High Priestess** suggests the development of the contemplative life, spiritual profundity, a heretofore unknown sensitivity, and an epiphany of man's place with woman and within the world. Yet the card often implies disengagement. It may indicate an ideal or dream woman, the anima, or soulmate.

- She alludes to what is hidden, intuition, perhaps even language itself. Yet she is silent.

- There is something sacred about her, something scared, something strange and estranged. She suggests a home of her making into which she cannot enter, a mouth without a tongue. She may be linked with the true expression of the Law.

III. THE EMPRESS ELIZABETH DICKENS

CHARACTER: Mrs. Catherine Nickleby

ROMAN À CLEF: Elizabeth Dickens

BOOK: *Nicholas Nickleby*

NOTES FOR GENERAL CIRCULATION:

- **The Empress** holds a picture of Queen Victoria, representing dominion over the Earth and her age. The queen is young, representing fertility and beauty, while the Empress is matronly, representing authority and experience.
- The fruits and vegetables signify the fecundity of nature. That they hang from the air suggests manna from heaven, bounty, and benevolence generally, and perhaps humanity's unwise exaltation of earthly pleasures above those of the higher spiritual plane.

- The prelapsarian Eden is strongly suggested. A kind of bliss is denoted, as is an ambivalence between innocence and ignorance.

- The washing hung to dry suggests domesticity and the mundane realities of life. As **The Empress** looks away from **The High Priestess**, the sheets may be those seen loose and sprawling there, cut, dried, and sanitized here. **The Empress** looks blithely toward **The Emperor**, whom she adores and defers to.

- **The Empress** card suggests and ease and feeling of being at home in the natural world—a natural world cultivated, tamed, and housebroken. She appears to be a dignified balance of humility and self-respect.

- The produce on display may allude to a trade-off, or commerce. In this way it forms a bond with **The Magician** and **The Emperor**, underscored by the real-life child and parent dynamic these three cards denote.

- In a formal pattern, **The Empress** alludes to comprehension, familial ties, a lack of practicality, the distaff, coquettish vanity, felicity, frivolity, kindness, manners, and the various levels of comprehension.

IV. THE EMPEROR JOHN DICKENS

CHARACTER: Wilkins Micawber

ROMAN À CLEF: John Dickens

BOOK: *David Copperfield*

NOTES FOR GENERAL CIRCULATION:

- **The Emperor** is counterpart to **The Empress** and represents man as he might be. He signifies an ascendancy or immunity over base material concerns.
- The walking stick he holds cuts the box circumscribing him in half, suggesting his refusal to allow his thoughts to be dragged down by the limitations of the physical world. That said, the walking stick may also suggest **The**

Emperor's reliance on the ground and his need of it to help keep him upright.

- The square, which boxes Micawber, suggests the four elements that frame man's existence. Their inadequate and unequal distribution is indicated by the hardship and deprivation of the Victorian commonwealth lurking in the card's background. In this way, the incredible affluence of the British Commonwealth itself is given a frame of reference. Micawber's back to this dark reality and his glib expression belie civilization's neglect and rejection of the ramifications of its own physical construct. Consider the care he takes with his gloves, so as not to soil his hands.

- In a formal pattern, **The Emperor** may indicate an authority of sorts, might like a windfall appear to assist you, must be contended with, or may become an unavoidable irritation.

- **The Emperor** and **The Empress** look in the same direction, toward Britain's Great Exhibition and accepted superego authority of **The Hierophant / Public Mores**.

- Traditional divinatory interpretations of **The Emperor** card include willpower, mind over matter, material wealth or abject poverty (or both), an authoritative manner, litigiousness, perseverance, indefatigability, grave misrepresentation, unsinkable aplomb, hot air, dignity, and undue poise. He is sometimes known as the Gypsy King.

V. THE HIEROPHANT
SOCIAL MORES

CHARACTERS: Canon Septimus Crisparkle; the Reverend Mr. Stiggins

ROMAN À CLEF: George W. Robinson

BOOKS: *The Mystery of Edwin Drood*; *The Pickwick Papers*

NOTES FOR GENERAL CIRCULATION:

- **The Hierophant** is linked with instruction, indoctrination, power, and authority. As with all cards numbered 5 in the Tarot, it signifies conflict, the struggle to find balance in the essentially disparate realms of matter and soul.

- The two clerical vignettes represent the polarities of the letter of the law and spirit, male and female, active and passive, sun and moon, alpha and omega, the universal and the iota, God's omnipotence and man's free will.

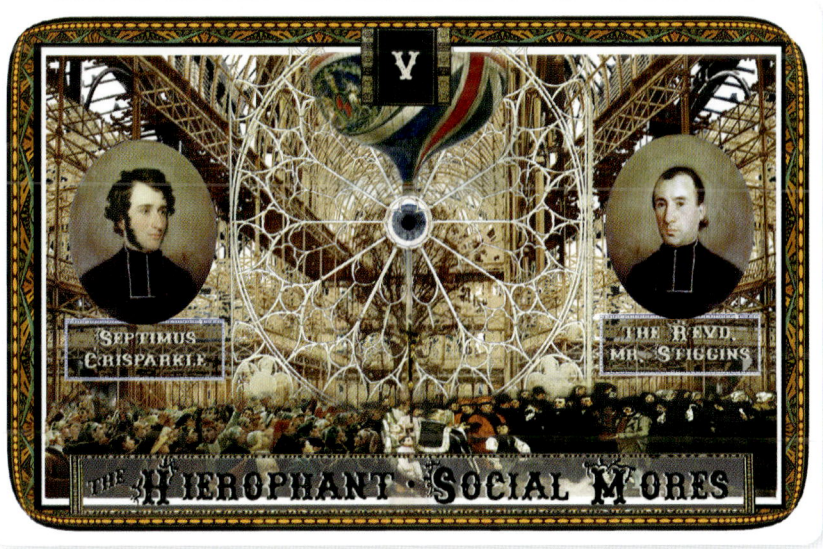

- The pontiff of traditional Tarot decks is replaced by the popeless eye of the populace—the Papal See replaced by what the people see, a bull's-eye made of the papal bull. Some affiliate **The Hierophant** with the zodiacal sign Taurus, the bull. Some associate it with kowtowing, others with bullying. Some even interpret it in the colloquial sense, as a euphemism for *bullshit*, punctuated by the hot-air balloon emblazoned with the Union Jack.

- **The Hierophant**, **The Devil**, **The Moon**, and **The Sun** cards share a kind of kinship; together they form a stable, four-cornered cube, representing the elements, the four corners of the Earth, and the foundation stones of the house of God. With the inclusion of **The High Priestess** card—otherwise ostracized—at the cube's center, this five-card family forms a quincunx, as in the cinquefoil of heraldry. In this intentionally oblique manner the conveyed idea is of induction, what is shown to the pupil and what is kept hidden. In this, the clever or intuitive pupil may see the in-built contradiction inherent to esoteric understanding and institutionalized form.

- The eye of **The Hierophant** is all seeing—it both oversees all and is the small *I* of each individual consciousness.

- In a traditional pattern, **The Hierophant** can signify the use and abuse of authority, knowledge, censor, duty, and sex.

- Some may see in **The Hierophant** mortification of the flesh, denial of the self, submission, prostration, and exhibitionism. Others may detect circumcision, an all-male Eden, and the subliminal presence of the "one-eyed snake."

VI. LOVERS CATHERINE HOGARTH, CHARLES DICKENS

CHARACTERS: Mr. Crummles as Friar Lawrence; Juliet; Romeo; Mrs. Capulet

ROMAN À CLEF: Catherine Hogarth; Charles Dickens; Georgina Hogarth *the elder*

BOOK: *Nicholas Nickleby*

NOTES FOR GENERAL CIRCULATION:

- Represents choice and decision. Suggests the movement from childhood to maturity, where the paradigms of parents are assumed by the child. The old *anima* and *animus*—seen in **The Empress** and **The Emperor**—must burgeon

anew in the young bud. What the choice actually is operates on numerous levels—between passivity and action, happiness and sorrow, self-gratification and familial support, reality and illusion.

- The image links with *Romeo & Juliet*, a play about past mistakes that a young couple attempts to break free from but end up only recasting. There may be implied a clash of good and bad in the surrender either to basic instincts or societal demands; which is good and which is bad remains unclear. It may be noted that the last card, **Public Mores**, as endorsed by the church and state, lies in the direction of the past. That the characters of Romeo and Juliet are but players, who strut and fret their hour upon the stage, suggests the people behind their roles are merely acting a part, reciting an author's dialogue. What appears Right may only be stage right—or what's left. This may suggest that the true understanding needed to make a wise decision must come from within a person rather than some imposed persona. Or perhaps a person must actually develop a part within their psyche, which acts as an audience to their condition. In this way, another allows for another, which allows one to see oneself. This is where human desires come in—we know Juliet will choose Romeo, and Romeo, Juliet, as surely as biology or fate. By not choosing sorrow, for example, represented by Lady Capulet, Romeo chooses the solar rather than the lunar influence, which is to say he adheres to his nature, and it all ends in tears.

- That said, many children are born of this union—both literal and literary. Therefore, perhaps a necessary cleaving of oneself to found and fecundate an inner unity is implied.

- In a formal pattern, **The Lovers** indicates the need for responsible action, well-meaning feelings, and a benign sense of doing right by another. On a deeper level, the card indicates the inner struggle to find the center of gravity between the sacred and profane, to honestly fathom one's own nature, and to reach an accord between society's expectations and our own core needs.

VII. THE CHARIOT
PUBLIC READINGS

ROMAN À CLEF: Charles Dickens

NOTES FOR GENERAL CIRCULATION:

- The seventh Major Arcanum represents man as he might be, what he is in the theater of his own soul; it is a kind of monologue. As a person's inner persona, it is a counterpart and commentary on the previous card, **The Lovers**.

- A theatrical production in which the central role has been tailor-made for the lead actor is commonly called a vehicle.

- Here, on **The Chariot** card, the rapt audience replaces the emotional pull of the horses on traditional **Chariot** cards. Dickens the public reader, as charioteer, maintains control over his audience's emotional energies with a deft hand. Balancing comedy with tragedy, he transports the audience.

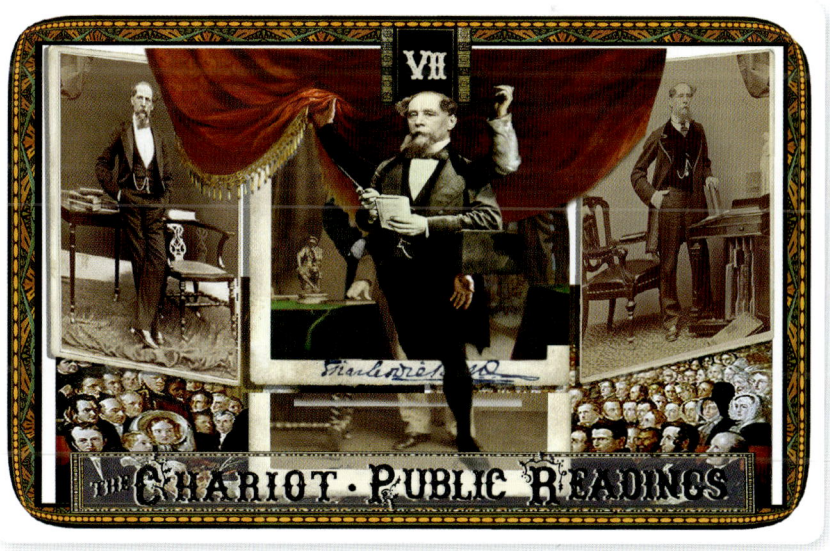

- **The Chariot** is the outward discipline of the Ego; it represents ideal agency, the perfected development of faculties, a sense of purpose and direction, the authoritative mastery of superego and id.

- This is the image of the idealized Everyman—what **The Magician** on paper is in practice. The charioteer has corralled all his solar energies and, as all things to all people, enacts them to great effect in the world. With a focus so intense, however, he runs the risk of forgetting to replenish his lunar energies. Acting in this way—in the heady and headlong gallop of willpower—may end with the charioteer crashing to the ground like Phaethon.

- **The Chariot** is affiliated with the star sign Sagittarius, the half human, half horse. As signified by Chiron, Sagittarians are natural teachers. Enjoying the sound of their own voice, they may become half hoarse. As with other **Fire** signs, they are easily bored and move quickly from one idea to another. They may be promiscuous. As archers, they can accurately zero in on a target from a sometimes disturbing distance.

- For the purposes of acting out his novels, Dickens often reduced incidents in his books to the dialogue alone, thereby eliminating himself from the work, as it were. When Dickens, performing his monopolylogues, carried his audiences away, where did *he* go?

- May suggest a concord of inner and outer desires. In a formal pattern, a female querent may find herself sidelined by a male in her life's career, while a male querent may be trapped in a role or addicted to something that brings solace but is ultimately detrimental to his health. Similarly, a third party may be almost miraculously moved, but at the cost of the loss of their transportation.

VIII. STRENGTH
GEORGINA HOGARTH

CHARACTER: Georgina Hogarth

ROMAN À CLEF: Georgina Hogarth; Charles Dickens

NOTES FOR GENERAL CIRCULATION:

- The eighth Major Arcanum represents the focus and control of animal instincts and their transmutation.

- The younger Georgina Hogarth is clipping the nails of the English lion, Charles Dickens. Allusion is made to the *Androcles & the Lion* myth and Daniel in the lions' den.

- The **Strength** card is the proper female counterpart to **The Magician** card.

- Georgina is neither too gentle nor too firm; she both subjugates and is the symbol of willing subjugation; by being beneath, she transcends.

- The bunting is the St. George's cross, patron saint of England. This correlates to Georgina's Christian name and the strength of the British Empire.

- The traditional zodiac correspondence to the **Strength** card is Leo, symbolized by the lion—king of the jungle and ruler of the heart. Georgina, as virgin, may suggest Virgo, taming Dickens's pride, and cleaning up the chaotic mess the creative Leo leaves behind.

- Traditionally, occult teaching instructs that one must never attempt to change or destroy something one finds distasteful, but rather must attempt to transform or put it in its rightful place. Here, Charles Dickens and Georgina Hogarth effortlessly put each other in their rightful places.

- The **Strength** card's presence in a formal reading suggests the framework of the question posed may be risen above; that something of an inferior quality may be transmuted, transformed, or substituted for a higher form.

- The jute bow holding the framed photograph of the elderly Georgina forms a lemniscate, indicating the balanced solar and lunar aspects of the card. In this way, individuality and freedom are intimately linked with commonality and service. For the soul to shine, the material world must be groomed and ministered to.

IX. THE HERMIT
PHILIP PIRRIP

CHARACTERS: Philip Pirrip, a.k.a. Pip

BOOK: *Great Expectations*

NOTES FOR GENERAL CIRCULATION:

- Traditionally the simplest card of the Major Arcana, **The Hermit** of *The Charles Dickens Tarot* is, like the novel representing it—*Great Expectations*—deceptively simple but decidedly complex.

- That which **The Hermit** is searching for, or from which he is trying to escape, is a matter of perspective, contingent on the position it holds within a formal pattern.

- As with the layers of an onion, or the concentric rings rippling on the water's surface, **The Hermit's** meaning is layered, requiring the reader to peel it

back. It is affiliated astrologically with Saturn, which governs limitations and fixed attitudes. The presence of **The Hermit** card calls on the reader to open up, allow others in, and let their true feelings out.

- The sunlight on the card is on the left, or the past, whereas the future resides in darkness and night. Pip, in the card's center, as the Major Arcanum who has made himself a minor card or pip, provides his own light. In the lantern of the Rider/Waite, **Hermit** is a Star of David; here, we may wonder if it's not Estella [Latin: *star*]. As the alchemist Martin Ruland said: "Imagination is the star in man." The sun and moon are within Pip's lamp, suggestive of the lemniscate, and implying that he has brought the outside world in. It may also suggest that from within the furnace of his own soul he forges the outside world. The young Pip looks directly at us, but his arms seem to be those of an older man.

- The presence of **The Hermit** card in a formal pattern indicates a need for liberation, a call to recognize the mistakes of the past and eschew the illusions one toils under in order that the new, the future, may be embraced. **The Hermit** may suggest a search, but this is more likely an illusion, a disavowal of the truth, or a self-deception. More often it is a clear indication that the reader must alter their attitude, because—consciously or not—this attitude is blocking their spiritual progress.

- Sometimes, **The Hermit** implies social death, exile, a rejection of the mayic world of illusion. One may believe that a retreat from the world is compensatory and corrective, but recall the trouble this caused the guilty, expectant Pip. In this sense, the card may indicate avarice, an uninquiring personality, the rejection of love, and misanthropy. Properly speaking, however, **The Hermit** indicates a balance of the demands of the outer world with those of the inner self, which achieves transcendence to another plane.

X. THE WEAL OF FORTUNE

CHARACTERS: Barnaby Rudge; Grip [raven]; Dolly Varden; Lord George Gordon

ROMAN À CLEF: Lord George Gordon

BOOK: *Barnaby Rudge*

NOTES FOR GENERAL CIRCULATION:

• The tenth card of the Major Arcana is the first card in the renewed decimal cycle; as such, it represents change, regeneration, and cyclical action. The number itself is made up of one and nothing. The Roman numeral X may suggest the multiplication or *times* sign, the mark on a treasure map, the mark on a ballot, how one signs their name if unable to write, the symbol indicating error as on a test, a crossroads, or Christ and his cross.

- Barnaby Rudge, the novel's namesake, has fallen to the ground, as though his hopes have been dashed. His simpleminded nature indicates his inability to learn from his experiences. His hat is festooned with the colorful plumes of a peacock, in stark contrast to the black profile of his pet raven, Grip. The former suggests humanity's adorning itself with vainglorious symbols of fancy, while the latter implies the tamed black animal that relinquishes the freedom of flight.

- As Barnaby is on the ground, Lord Gordon holds a half-circle hat, has one foot on a book, and points toward the ground. Dolly Varden is in the center of the card, on the ascendant, in her hand a key indicating her father's vocation, her importance, and Barnaby's freeing from prison.

- Soldiers in King George's army on the left side of the **Weal** card shoot indiscriminately into the crowd of May Pole revelers on the right side of the card.

- The material plane of the card is seemingly chaotic while, behind everything, Time proceeds mechanically.

- The traditional divinatory meaning of the **Weal** card suggests a period of instability, uncertainty, and impermanence. On a superficial level, this suggests the vicissitudes of fashion.

- As the eye of a storm is still, so the hub of *Master Humphrey's Clock*—about which the tale of *Barnaby Rudge* revolves—is obscured by the half-shut eye of Dolly Varden. Directly above this, on Barnaby's overturned basket crowning Dolly, is the stark white eye of Grip. Together, these images may suggest the lunar-mercurial aspects at work in the card, calling on a balanced center of gravity if man is to remain on course.

- The word *weal* means happiness, prosperity, the assessment of the quality of life and general well-being of individuals and societies as a whole. A *weal* is also a raised mark on the body, caused by a blow, as from a rod or a whip.

XI. JUSTICE CHANCERY

CHARACTERS: Miss Flite; Inspector Bucket;
Richard Carstone; Ada Clare

ROMAN À CLEF: Inspector Charles Frederick Field

BOOK: *Bleak House*

NOTES FOR GENERAL CIRCULATION:

- The **Justice** card represents a warning and indicates a need for proper deliberation.
- Affiliated with the astrological sign Libra, **Justice** is involved with inner questioning. One of the major difficulties faced by Librans is coming to a decision.

- The Lord Justice in wig and full judicial resplendence looks out, over the heads and beyond the immediate everyday realities of the litigants beneath him. His gaze is august, practiced, and immutable. He audits all that has gone before, his back turned resolutely to what's coming—the injustice of **The Hanged Man**, where the ruling is death.

- The edifice of the courthouse is decaying. Miss Flite's birds will die in their cages, waiting for Judgment Day. They are miner's canaries for Richard Carstone, who will die poor having gotten nowhere.

- The presence of the **Justice** card in a formal pattern may suggest an obsession with a detail, which can never be made fine enough, an uncertainty that can never be proven, a wrong that will never be made right.

- Ostensibly, the **Justice** card signifies man's law and his assumed sovereignty over the Earth, its inhabitants, its future. It is almost all letter and next to no spirit.

- On a more personal note, **Justice** suggests each individual's conscience—the human capability to divine good from evil and its attendant responsibility.

XII. THE HANGED MAN
SYDNEY CARTON

CHARACTER: Sydney Carton

BOOK: *A Tale of Two Cities*

NOTES FOR GENERAL CIRCULATION:

- **The Hanged Man** is a commentary on the conflict between humanity's inner state and the world they have constructed for themselves. Sydney Carton is a prisoner, confined in a cell, surrounded by death. When a free man, his inner life had not been much different. Here, he is in a lonely, uncomfortable position, yet his posture reflects a blasé and untroubled attitude and his face shows little real concern.
- **The Hanged Man** is a card representing a standstill reached between the immovable object and the irresistible force: the Ascendant first house of Selfhood and the Descendant seventh house sometimes called the house of marriage. The severed heads and skulls signify matter divested of vivifying spirit, while Carton's defiant act of self-sacrifice is both an exoneration of and a testament to the invisible life force.

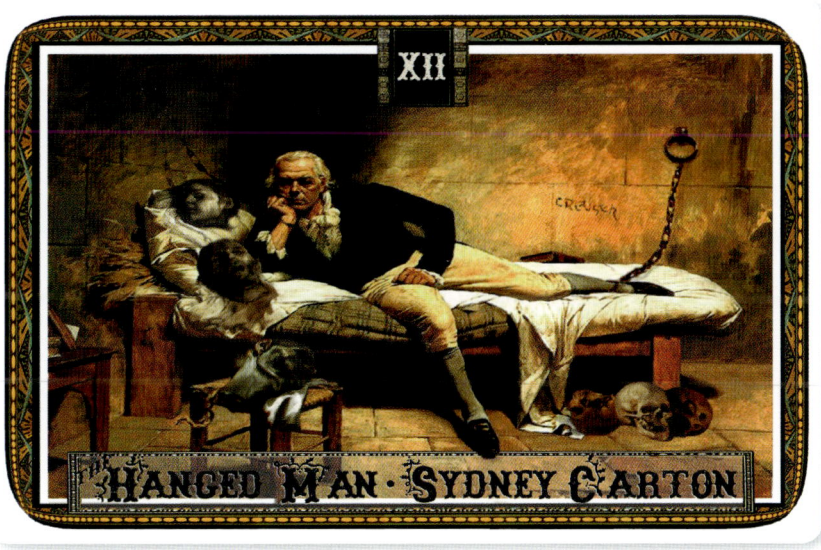

- Traditional divinatory meanings of **The Hanged Man** vary greatly and include The Law of Man versus The Rules of the Universe, epiphany, redemption, transcendence, a miraculous solution, the unconscious made manifest, ego death, psychosis, and a crucible culminating in the collision between the reality of the unconscious and the unconsciousness of reality.
- The card is the meeting place of ironies, the birthplace of paradox—the best of times, the worst of times. Insofar as it is an incident that occurred in the past, it shows that human life as it is now being lived is upside down, inside out, unnatural—time out of joint. Here, by choosing death, **The Hanged Man** chooses life. By setting *A Tale of Two Cities* in the past, Dickens suggests a crisis that is perpetual.
- By setting *A Tale of Two Cities* in a country other than England, Dickens begins a symbolic journey of expansion that sees fruition on **The World** card. In this cell exists the entire world, and like a cell—the fundamental building block of life—it divides, multiplies, and expands.
- As Sydney Carton and Charles Darnay are in a sense twins, they represent Jesus Christ and Judas Iscariot. Many Gnostics believed Judas was an instrument of Divine Wisdom, a *daimon*, which means both demon and angel, making his betrayal of Jesus a victory over the material world. The card's skulls suggest Golgotha. The French word scratched into the wall, *creuser*, is the imperative verb *dig*. Like the word INRI inscribed atop Christ's crucifix, it signifies God's word—the word made flesh. To dig is to unearth and to understand. The card's name suggests Judas's suicide by hanging, while Iscariot can mean "the false one," "the assassin" [itself a binate word; compare *The Golden Ass*], and the verb tense "to deliver" with its double entendre: to bring about and to remove life. Despite or because of questions concerning free will, both Judas and Jesus are bound up in the fulfillment of God's purpose.
- In the end, the outer crisis demands an inner solution. Sydney Carton is a symbol of the crossroads of physical reality and cosmic truth; namely, man must die in order to be reborn.
- By performing the ultimate sacrifice for the greater good, Dickens achieves through Sidney Carton both a more personal and a more universal balance with the forces of evil than conceivable in the **Justice** card. In Dickens's own real-life predicament, he achieved equilibrium between the outward demands of his time and place and the inner necessities of his emotional and spiritual life.
- The French Revolution's Law of Suspects and subsequent Reign of Terror are intimated as the follow-on from the previous card, **Justice**, a link underscored by the lawyer Carton's shackled pose in its direction. Judas was replaced as the twelfth Apostle, making him the thirteenth—an allusion to the twelfth house of the zodiacal figure, the house of *karma*, and the card that is to follow: the 13th, **Death**.

XIII. DEATH MARY HOGARTH

CHARACTER: Little Nell

ROMAN À CLEF: Mary Hogarth

BOOK: *The Old Curiosity Shop*

NOTES FOR GENERAL CIRCULATION:

- Traditionally the unnamed card of the Major Arcana, **Death** in *The Charles Dickens Tarot*, goes unnumbered, like the thirteenth floor of most buildings. It may be noted that a year with thirteen full moons instead of twelve was a problem for the monks in charge of calendars, since it upset the normal arrangement of church festivals. The solar calendar is also at odds with the lunar calendar, which sees thirteen lunar cycles a year, not to mention a woman's thirteen commensurate menstrual cycles a year. It may also be worth noting that the thirteenth card in traditional Tarot decks is the Queen—or here, in *The Charles Dickens Tarot*, the **Mother**.

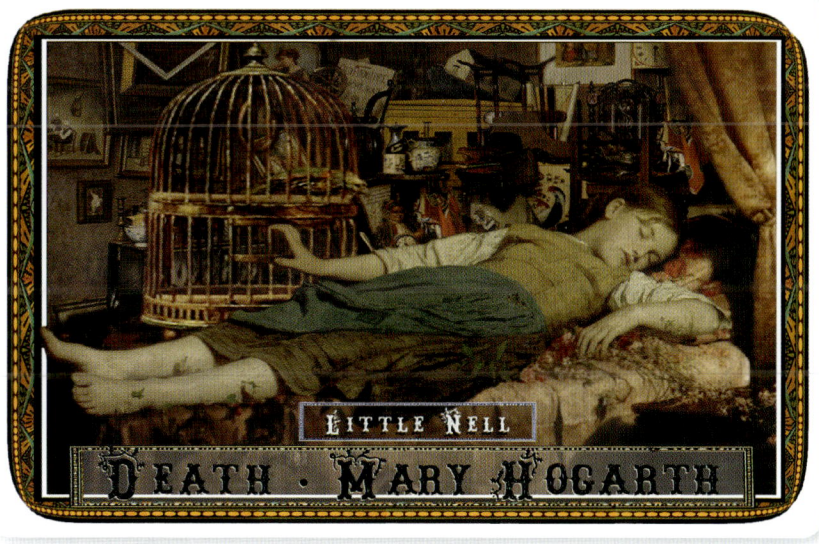

- Little Nell's caged parrot represents her incarcerated spirit, and the emancipating aspect of **Death**, as attended to by the Paraclete. The bird's cage may suggest the human skeletal system, ruled by Capricorn.

- The disparity between the still, supine body of Little Nell and the clamor of the Old Curiosity Shop's unwanted junk signifies the disparity between the soul and inanimate matter. The stockpile of antique keepsakes looming over Nell represents the dangers of holding to the past, to material items as attempted talisman against impending and inevitable **Death**. These material goods call into question the true nature of gain.

- The flowers may suggest Rose Maylie, a character fated to die, which Dickens was unable to brave.

- The name Nell, an endearment of the name Ellen, is a homophone for *knell*—from Old English *cnyll*—to toll a bell slowly, to resound, to signal, to proclaim, to summon, especially at a funeral.

- The name Agnes means "pure" and "holy" and is the name of one of the four virgin martyrs; it cognates with the Latin word *agnus*, meaning "lamb." This suggests that the tension built up in the card's background may demand some kind of sacrifice.

- Little Nell's death is fictional, suggesting metaphysical change and the very real need for transformation. On a deeper level, the **Death** card suggests a way of clearing away the deadwood, vivifying what has grown lifeless, and letting the dead bury the dead. Deeper still, by surrendering what one holds dear, something greater, more real, and more sublime is born.

- That **Death** is represented by a young woman and girl indicates the card's underlying message of regeneration and fertility, echoed in the card's traditional association with the Hebrew letter *Mem*, meaning "fountain," "spring," "tongue," and "God's fecundity." This aspect of *Mem*, meaning in its simplest form "water," associates **Death** with the zodiacal sign of fixed **Water**, Scorpio—the region in which spirit, unable to find expression, must remain until it is exorcised through regeneration. In this way, the **Death** card forms a unique bond with the card bereft of life-giving **Water** and which, seen backward, is the past tense of *live*—**The Devil**. The nature of this bond is a circuit, one that cannot be broken until **Death**, like the Phoenix reborn of its ashes, makes its regenerative sacrifice. This may indicate that the interstitial card, **Temperance**, with its moderation and amelioration, may be misguided or counterproductive. **Death** is also locked in an almost alchemical bond with the essential card of mutable **Water: The High Priestess.**

XIV. TEMPERANCE FACT/ FICTION

CHARACTERS: Cecilia "Sissy" Jupe; Signor Jupe

ROMAN À CLEF: Angela Burdett-Coutts

BOOKS: *Hard Times*; *Household Words*; *All The Year Round*; *The Uncommercial Traveller*

NOTES FOR GENERAL CIRCULATION:

- The **Temperance** card is something of an intermediary between the **Death** and **The Devil** card. It signifies the balance between the spirit's emancipation from life and the worldly trappings of living.

- The binary poles of *Hard Times* constitute the fusion of opposites in **Temperance**—fact and fiction, factory and circus, schoolroom and experience. This dichotomy is made literal in *Hard Times'* title: the Latin root *temp* means time, while, in metallurgy, to *temper* is to render hard through heating.

- The boy and girl of the **Temperance** card allude to the boy—Want—and girl—Ignorance—of the ensuing **Devil** card. Their sex being poles themselves, these children are being pulled along together toward their destiny by a kind of angel—Angela Burdett-Coutts, 1st Baroness Burdett-Coutts, the "richest heiress in England"—another clear contradistinction with the **Devil/Poverty** card.

- As with the three central figures, the **Temperance** card is divided into three. While all manifestations are essentially triadic, the third dialectical force remains invisible to the sublunary plane, where it is possible to perceive only the duality of negative and positive forces.

- The flow of dark forces toward the light, from the fictitious Coketown to the Sleary Circus, suggests a melting—or perhaps smelting—of transient emotional energies from the subconscious to the hardened energies of the conscious intellectual mind—a circularity of forces akin to the yin and yang fishes.

- The central figure in flowing garments suggests spiritual agency. She is the Maiden of the zodiac, Virgo, involved with the critical assessment of material facts in order to arrive at truth. As Miss Coutts, she is the unwed virgin protectress of "fallen" women. As Demeter, she is Persephone's mother—two aspects of the triple goddess—the giver of food and the bringer of the sacred law.

- **Temperance** is affiliated with the Hebrew letter *Nun*, a palindrome meaning fish and suggesting nun—a vestal priestess, from the Persian *nana*, meaning mother and tutor. Coming between **Death** and **The Devil**, it may suggest the noon of midday.

- **Temperance** can be linked with *Nut*, Egyptian guardian of the shades of the dead. This in turn suggests *nut*, signifying fruit and the seeds of the Eleusinian Mysteries, as well as *nub*, as in kernel, and *nubile*.

- **Temperance** is associated with Mary, the Mother of God; more, she is the Christian tripartite Martha, Mary Magdalene, and Virgin Mary.

- In mythology, **Temperance** is affiliated with Iris, goddess of the sea and sky—emotion and thought. She is messenger between man and the gods, and the personification of the rainbow. A rainbow is the result of a fusion between water and light, with the physical liquid wave dividing the intangible fluorescent wave into its constituent parts—or, the white light, which illumines the blackness transformed into the full spectrum of color, including those invisible to the naked eye. In this way, **Temperance** is the balance between **Fire, Air,** and **Water**—**Fire** combusting in **Air** to give light, light passing through **Water** to create the rainbow. Fittingly, the iris is the eye's color and is responsible for controlling the pupil.

XV. THE DEVIL POVERTY

CHARACTERS: Fagin; Ignorance; Want; Oliver Twist

BOOK: *Oliver Twist*

NOTES FOR GENERAL CIRCULATION:

- **The Devil** represents stagnation, material frustration, hindrances to moral development, and, finally, the barriers to spiritual emancipation.
- Rather than depict **The Devil** himself, whose role is easily misinterpreted, the central representational figure on **The Devil** card is obscure. The characters in *Oliver Twist* are as the layers of an onion or the Stations of the Cross—they lead one regressively from Oliver to Noah Claypool to the Artful Dodger to Fagin to Bill Sykes to Monks. It will be remembered that much of Oliver Twist's misfortune is in actuality orchestrated from the shadows by Oliver's own half brother, Monks. This enigmatic, nefarious figure represents the malevolent aspects inherent in the fraternity of man—his very epithet, Monks, being a black joke on the reclusive religious order of brothers.
- The two figures on either side of the card, and the male and female children, draw an affiliation among **The Lovers**, **Temperance**, and **The Devil** cards. Choices bound up in the sixth Arcanum may become as the bondage of the

fifteenth. The fourteenth Arcanum may attempt to ameliorate the manacles of duality, or it may indeed reveal that what in the beginning seemed to be choices were in the end not choices at all. As written on the forehead of *Want*, Doom may be sponged from the stone, for these are not the shadows of things that Will be, but the shadows of things that May be, only. In this way, the dialectic of these three cards May be seen in the twentieth Arcanum: **Judgment**.

- In the smoke-choked maze of London streets, which forms **The Devil** card's background, the elements **Fire**, **Air**, and **Earth** are represented, but not **Water**. The undine element is missing precisely because it loosens, refreshes, dissolves; **The Devil XV Poverty** card represents rigidity, rigor mortis, the state of being insensate—it is in desperate want of **Water**, essential symbol of life itself.

- Oliver and Fagin, on either side of **The Devil** card, suggest the penitent and impenitent thieves of Christ's Crucifixion. That two males supplant the traditional male/female dichotomy of the fifteenth Arcanum highlights the principally male aspect of incarceration and impasse **The Devil** represents. The obscured angelic figure and the children she shields highlight man's conflation of sexual neurosis and Original Sin, symbolized in the novel by the disgrace and obfuscation surrounding Oliver's birth.

- On the literal, superficial, mundane plane, **The Devil** indicates the disruption and corruption of character, loss of power and money, and a reduction to animal subsistence. On a deeper, more accurate level, **The Devil** represents stagnation, deadlock, obstruction, vexation, and a sense of insuperable spiritual ostracism. As the ensuing sixteenth Arcanum card implies, something has to give before even one more step can be taken.

- Only through sacrifice or suffering can regeneration occur. Thus, **The Devil**, reaching here an impasse, is sent back to the **Death** card. It will be remembered that Mary Hogarth died while Dickens was writing *Oliver Twist*. The character of Oliver's angelic aunt Rose Maylie is homage to Mary Hogarth. Dickens contrived to have Rose Maylie fall deathly ill, but he could not bring himself to kill her. Instead, this death would have to wait until Little Nell Trent, whose name and nature are a clear allusion to Nelly Ternan, **The High Priestess.**

- Superficially, **The Devil** is affiliated with Taurus, the most material of the zodiacal signs. This creates a fraternity between **The Devil** and **The Hierophant**. Where there was putatively displayed transparency and pride, here the veil is rent to reveal Stygian obscurity and abasement. On a deeper, more accurate level, **The Devil** is affiliated with Taurus's polarity, Scorpio, where **Water** stagnates, intentions remain incomplete, truths stay half true, lies fester, and frustrations fetter the soul. All crimes and deficiencies of spirit are contained within the Scorpionic domain, awaiting regeneration through self-sacrifice. This, symbolized by the universality of the crawling crustacean, is Scorpio's damnation; seen in its highest symbol the sole Phoenix, it is Scorpio's salvation.

XVI. THE TOWER
STAPLEHURST

ROMAN À CLEF: Charles Dickens; Ellen Ternan; Frances Ternan

NOTES FOR GENERAL CIRCULATION:

- Traditional interpretations of the sixteenth card of the Major Arcana see it signifying catastrophe and physical or mental illness. The card's traditional name, *The House of God*, was a colloquial name for a hospital in the Middle Ages.

- Trains represent a series of events, the unstoppable progress of modernity. The gap in the bridge of the Staplehurst Disaster suggests a hole in Charles Dickens's life he was unable to span. Regardless of the regulations in place and the careful administration of precautions, accidents and the unforeseen will occur, no matter how thorough and well thought out man's protocols are.

- The carriages of a train, although linked together, can also be regarded for all intents and purposes as separate. The engine, the brake van, the first- and second-class coaches and travelers—all imply the discrete compartmentalization and packaging the human mind devises to quantify, divide, and evaluate the stream of Time.

- Often likened to the Tower of Babel, the horizontal aspect of **XVI The Tower Staplehurst** card represents the lapidary horizontal procession of words, as across the pages of a book, from the mind of an author writing—or rewriting— his life story.

- **The Tower** may indicate a sexual tension or impasse that has reached a climax; trains are commonly used as symbols for sex. In dream analysis, trains are said to symbolize fear in male dreamers and the phallus in female dreamers. Traveling by train indicates that the dreamer is advancing too quickly through life; a gap in the rails suggests that the dreamer's life has gone off track.

- Dickens's levelheaded reaction to the Staplehurst Disaster and his subsequent PTSD indicate that no matter how heroic one's response to catastrophe may be, the circle cannot be squared, or vice versa. A man is made up of mind and body, head and heart, self and other—the two both live their own lives and are inseparable. When one grows to control and dominate the other, a hole forms in the bridge between them, to redress through rupture this corruption of the whole.

- Esoteric teaching, as seen on religious facades such as Reims Cathedral, holds that when the Holy Family fled from Herod and entered a pagan town, the unholy temples fell to the ground. Presumably, the spiritual power of the Holy Family was too great for the *genius loci* to withstand. In a formal reading, this interpretation implies that the reader has been unable to respond to life with sufficient understanding, humanity, or spiritual "being." The fabric of the veil has been rent. The lacuna can be filled only by the stone the masons threw away.

- Verticality indicates spiritual ascendance; the horizontal plane indicates the crisscrossing mundane worlds of intellect and emotion. **The Tower** card, then, with its lack or very limited vertical structure, indicates a crisis brought about by the paucity of spiritual advancement. More, the hegemony of the intellect, seen in the rapidly expanding railway system, gives way under its own weight and imperfection to the underlying realm of emotions, represented by the **Water** element of the River Beult.

- In short, **The Tower** represents a turning point in Dickens's control over his own narrative, a tearing asunder of his ability to marshal the demands of his head and his heart, his public and private lives. This is a personal, spiritual dilemma—not, as the Staplehurst Disaster might imply, simply an earthly one. As such, **The Tower** indicates a personal apogee or crunch for the reader.

XVII. THE STAR
GAD'S HILL

ROMAN À CLEF: Mamie Dickens; Charles Dickens; Kate Dickens

NOTES FOR GENERAL CIRCULATION:

- Represents inspiration, creative release, redemption, grace, nourishment, and the soul at ease.
- The pitchers of the traditional **Star** card are replaced by a picture of Gad's Hill and a picture of filial devotion in Dickens and his daughters' portrait. His two daughters at his side may suggest an association between creative energies and sexual energies.
- The lush countryside behind emphasizes the idea of growth. The small patch of water indicates the easy flow of creative juices and iterates the idea of sustenance.
- As Dickens's dream home, Gad's Hill represents the fulfillment of a wish or

a hard-won accomplishment. As the Dickens home, Gad's Hill represents the inspiration and comfort Dickens drew from time spent with family and entertaining friends. As the location of a key incident in Shakespeare's life and work, Gad's Hill represents a well-deserved inheritance, a fertile heritage, and an inspired line of transmission. With its Swiss chalet aerie, Gad's Hill represents a haven, a windfall, a sanctum sanctorum.

- Dickens's writing made him a star. His stardom allowed him to purchase the house he visualized owning as a boy. Here, he wrote some of his greatest works. The suggestion may be then that inspirational forces are heaven born, and that the twinkling stars that quicken the inert matter in man ask in recompense only that man in emulation inject into inert matter a similarly shared life force through the making of works of art.

- In Tarot tradition, the specific star alluded to is Sirius, which marks the Dog Days of summer. Dickens lived at Gad's Hill in the twilight of his life; the exuberant, boyish author had become remarkably serious in middle age. Dickens's daughters on either side of him—one headstrong, the other melancholy—may allude to the two women on the upcoming **Moon** card, aspects represented on standard Tarot decks by dogs.

- Dickens's time at Gad's Hill corresponds to his separation from his wife and the thirteen-year affair he maintained in secret with Ellen Ternan. It underscores the author's ability to balance his business and literary life with his domestic family life and the demands of a mistress who lived for some time in France. In this way, **The Star** card represents harmony and an even distribution of various conflicting elements.

- Dickens's children both symbolize the fictional children he created, representing man's ethereal legacy, and his flesh and blood progeny, representing man's earthly legacy. Both indicate a fecundity and kind of rebirth.

- Dickens's conscious life began in Chatham, and it ended there. Having begun his literary career as **The Magician**, he ends it in the Star of the Magi, the Christmas Star, with his children around him in a reverse nativity.

XVIII. THE MOON
THE MYSTERY

CHARACTERS: Edwin Drood; Rosa Bud; Helena Landless; Neville Landless

BOOK: *The Mystery of Edwin Drood*

NOTES FOR GENERAL CIRCULATION:

- The eighteenth card of the Major Arcana represents the spirit in the material world. This may be a Hell on Earth, or but a dream within a dream.
- The dove represents hope and the Holy Spirit—the true female aspect of the Christian Trinity. The false female aspect is the church—the so-called Bride of Christ—a misogynist structure built and maintained by men. The hard-stone reality of the fictional Cloisterham Cathedral has little reality here on **The Moon** card. Of some note is the meaning of *cloister*—to shut up or secret away. Also, the *cloister* of a church is a covered arcade used for walking meditation, usually a four-sided circuit surrounding an open area of nature and dedicated to the Virgin Mary.

- The main figures on the left and right suggest light and dark, good and bad, west and east—the exact allocation of each depends on one's vantage. They may also suggest other dualities, such as male and female, civilized and savage, awake and asleep, living and dead, or simply duality itself. It may be worth noting that the two women are both in the foreground and wear white, whereas the men wear black and remain in the background like shadows. Rosa appears to be somnambulant, while Helena looks intently out at the reader.
- **The Moon** card, as emblematic of the **Water** signs, bears an intimate kinship with the **Water** suit of the Minor Arcana, and the **High Priestess**, **The Chariot**, and the **Death** cards of the Majors. In many cultures, the moon is the Land of the Dead, the regenerating receptacle where souls journey to after their mortal body here on Earth returns to ash and dust.
- **The Moon** card is the female aspect of the male **Sun** card. Both are intrinsically bound up with the inner workings of the human psyche. As such, **The Sun** represents the ego and the conscious mind, while **The Moon** represents the id and the subconscious. **The Moon** also rules the world of dreams. The dark aspect of **The Moon** implies delusion, hallucination, lunacy, and all the monsters the sleep of reason produces.
- **The Moon** card presides over the formation of life as well as its decomposition; hence *The Mystery of Edwin Drood* is half formed and half finished. In a formal reading, **The Moon** card may indicate a pregnancy or a project that will have to be abandoned.
- Religious scholars had difficulty fitting the thirteen-month lunar cycle into their twelve-month solar calendar, with the result that 13 became an unlucky number and the moon became synonymous with inconsistency. Tellingly, it is the solar calendar that needs a day added every four years, and even then deviates.
- The female aspect of **The Moon** card makes it mistress over the **Water** and **Earth** suits. With dominion over **Water**, the moon regulates not only the ocean tides but the Earth's rains, symbolizing the quenching of the parched land. With dominion over **Earth**, the moon regulates man's connection to the animal world and the cycle of life. By cupping and returning the light of the sun to all living things in the darkness, **The Moon** indicates that in life, balance is needed and grace is at work in the world.
- **The Moon** is intimately linked with creativity. Creativity demands the death and destruction of matter to remake it anew. This is underscored by the death of Dickens, who died during the composition of *The Mystery of Edwin Drood*. He wished to be buried in a discreet grave on the grounds of Rochester Cathedral, the unfinished novel's locus. Instead, he was buried at Poet's Corner in London. There remains, to this day, in the Rochester Cathedral graveyard, an empty burial plot for Charles Dickens.

XIX. THE SUN
THE ATHENAEUM CLUB

CHARACTERS: John Podsnap; Thomas Idle

ROMAN À CLEF: John Forster; Wilkie Collins

BOOK: *The Life of Charles Dickens*

NOTES FOR GENERAL CIRCULATION:

- The nineteenth card of the Major Arcana indicates the outward moving, male-created world, epitomized in many ways by the British Empire of the nineteenth century.

- The sun is the vivifying aspect of life on Earth. As such, it animates the inanimate. Together with the female aspect of Water, signified in **The Moon** card, life is possible on this planet. Like the circadian rhythms of day and night, **The Sun** and **The Moon** work in harmony to sustain the Earth's cyclical, self-contained ecosystem, exemplified by **The Sun's** warmth evaporating the world's oceans, which in turn falls as rain on the land to make it fertile.

- Forster and Collins have their backs to **The Sun**, suggesting it is too blinding to look directly at. They have their backs to one another, suggesting they represent two aspects of male bonding—the conditional love of the father figure in Forster, and the liberating youthfulness of an adopted son in Collins.

- Gentlemen's clubs were private members-only clubs set up by and for British upper-class men in the eighteenth century and popularized by upper-middle-class men in the nineteenth century.

- Athena, who gives the Athenaeum its name, was the goddess of war, art, and rational thought.

- The male aspect of **The Sun** card makes it master over the **Fire** and **Air** suits. With dominion over **Fire**, the sun regulates the Earth's temperature and sparks life. With dominion over **Air**, the sun regulates the earth's atmosphere and its supply of light, facilitating photosynthesis. The sun gives us the day— God's first creation and man's inspiration for all his own subsequent dichotomies.

- **The Sun** represents the Ego and the rational mind, and all that strives and competes to succeed in man. Unchecked, it tends toward solipsism and hegemony, and its power can be overwhelmingly destructive. More often than not, its unchecked power is self-destructive.

XX. JUDGMENT
EBENEZER SCROOGE

CHARACTERS: Fan; Ebenezer Scrooge; Tiny Tim; Marley's ghost

BOOK: *A Christmas Carol*

NOTES FOR GENERAL CIRCULATION:

- The twentieth card of the Major Arcana is an allegory of spiritual rebirth. The scene is Christmas morning, and Scrooge has awoken from his bad sleep. He has shaken off his old life and the tomb, which no one will visit except to ridicule. In their place, Scrooge has embraced love, symbolized by becoming Tiny Tim's "second father" and carrying him on his shoulders.

- Some find grace naturally; others need help. Scrooge's visitation by Marley and the three ghosts "quickens" him, as with an epiphany, into a state of grace. This gift of insight and vision is a wake-up call, and the **Judgment** card represents just such a demand for total conversion.

- The darkness and alienation of the watery **Moon** card, together with the arid and extrovert intellectualization of **The Sun** card, when balanced, engender the creation of the soul. Tiny Tim, as child of man and woman, signifies this spiritual fruition. As it is Christmas morning, Tiny Tim can suggest the Christ child—the Son of Man, the Lamb of God, the Redeemer—who will himself be resurrected.

- Spirit of Tiny Tim, thy childish essence was from God! Much did thy loved ones learn from thee; much can the world learn of the nobility of patience from thy sweet child life. Unawares thou wert thyself an answer to thy Christmas prayer: "God bless us every one!"

- The **Judgment** card in a formal pattern indicates a successful conclusion, an act of benign generosity, an eleventh-hour *Volte-face*, a second chance, the importance of every action, the call to share the world's material riches, the crucial need to stay open and alive rather than closed and defensive no matter one's age, the dawning of hope after the darkness, a spiritual crisis, and the weakness of a seemingly indestructible evil.

XXI. THE WORLD

CHARACTERS: All

ROMAN À CLEF: Charles Dickens

BOOKS: All

NOTES FOR GENERAL CIRCULATION:

- The ultimate card of the Major Arcana is a culmination of all the preceding cards and as such is exceedingly difficult to ascribe with one specific meaning. Simply put, it is the *anima mundi*, the world soul; it is the egg of Charles Dickens's oeuvre, disseminated across not only the four corners of the Earth but across the fifth hidden dimension of time.

- The spinning globe, which circles the sun and which in turn is circled by the moon, creating the days, the seasons, the years, represents the universal lemniscate, the returning eternity of time itself. The globe, as a circle,

represents the perfect and never-ending, the entirety of everything and the zero of **The Fool**.

- A balance between the four elements has not only been achieved but utilized and potentiated to the greater—the greatest—good. This good is all inclusive, even of evil, for it is neither threatened nor in any way subordinate to evil, but rather in its perfection maintains control over all. **The Devil** is freed and **The Hanged Man** has become one with his other half. **The Hermit** no longer needs his crutch but has become himself the lantern, the light.

- Within the worldly plane, matter encapsulates and subjugates spirit; here, on **The World** card, the spirit is emancipated, which in turn emancipates matter. The individual, the one, is unified and made whole in the Absolute Being.

- The map of the world here on **The World** card is the center leaf of a book; the book represents Dickens's oeuvre, and the book, made from trees, represents the Tree of Life. The small inset or legend is a reduced version of the whole card, which, since it too contains a reduced version, creates a fractal, indicating the "as above, so below" of the macrocosm and the microcosm.

- The four stamps issued by the Royal Mail to celebrate Dickens's death and Literary Anniversary represent the traditional tetramorphs of **The World** card, in turn representing the four fixed signs of the zodiac, the four elements, and the four evangelists. The post aspect underscores the original dissemination of Dickens's works throughout the English-speaking world of the British Empire and beyond.

- The young Dickens of **The Magician** card has become Charles Dickens the accomplished author in his maturity. His eyes are closed as in meditation, receiving energy from across the four corners of the Earth and sending energy back out. **The World** card is sometimes called Truth or Wisdom.

- **The World** in traditional divination indicates the successful fulfillment of a dream; as a negative indicator, it suggests obstacles to one's aims or undue attachment to earthly matters.

EPILOGUE

THE FIGURE IN THE CARPET

The Charles Dickens Tarot (CDT) is not just a powerful working Tarot deck created for the purposes of divination, but also a study of all of Dickens's novels and a biographical introduction to the great man's life. Unlike the vertical orientation of most playing cards and Tarot decks, the CDT displays its images in a horizontal frame to resemble a theatrical stage or open book. Spread across the back of the CDT's cards is an oriental carpet, symbol of both exoticism and domesticity, decoration and practicality, and allusion to Victorian England's dominion across the globe. It also evokes the literary notion of "the figure in the carpet" from the novella of the same name by Henry James, indicating a meaningful image that suddenly stands out from the abstract patterns formed by a thousand separate threads. For a Tarot reading is, in essence, an attempt to identify a compelling, discursive narrative that similarly makes sense of many seemingly unrelated strands. The classic Rider-Waite-Smith deck, which provides the basic symbolic structure on which the CDT is constructed, derives much of its suggestive

complexity from the various occult systems woven into it. The CDT adds an even-greater density of interpretive possibilities by choosing emblematic images selected from the great tapestry of narratives that make up the novels and stories of Charles Dickens.

As a predictive oracle, the CDT offers unusually rich possibilities because the fate—or future—of the fictional character featured on each card is actually made explicit in the novel in which they appear. Details of their past are also part of the stories, as are their relationships with other characters and their relevance to Dickens's own life story. We can see where each person came from and where they are going. This can supply card readers with very specific information to inform the answers they give to clients' questions. For those who are not conversant with every nuance of Dickens's vast oeuvre, the companion book that comes with the deck provides synopses of the plots of all the novels, introduces the characters on each card, and places them within the context of established Tarot meanings.

At first glance, Dickens may not seem to have much in common with the occult nature of the Tarot. Though nominally an Anglican, and though he wrote a brief condensation of the New Testament for his young children, called *The Life of Our Lord*, Dickens paid little attention either in his life or fiction to formal religion. However, during his lifetime Dickens was the most famous and revered writer in the world, a moral touchstone for millions, and his continuing popularity establishes him as a reliable source of wisdom and a trustworthy spiritual guide, granting his novels the status of modern myths. We still recognize in them our common humanity, our collective unconscious, and the enduring core dynamics of human relationships.

A distinctive feature resulting from the alignment of Tarot archetypes with Dickens's work is the recurring configuration of family matters. Dickens himself had a large family and was an outspoken proponent of familial bonds. His era was one of increased domesticity, and the Victorians struggled with the burgeoning idea of romantic love and their own ornate structures of society and human relation. Unlike many of his own novels, Dickens was unable to live happily ever after within his own marriage—he and his wife underwent a very public separation, and, for the last thirteen years of his life, Dickens maintained a very secret relationship with Ellen Ternan, a girl half his age. This reality, scrupulously bowdlerized from Dickens's public persona, is woven into the Major Arcana of the CDT, as are the key components of Dickens's life. Many of Dickens's family and friends inspired characters in his works, and their inclusion in the trump cards in turn inspires an added layer of depth and gravity to the deck.

To demonstrate the deck in action, we shall suppose that Dickens himself comes to the CDT with two questions. The first involves a key moment in his life when he was toiling to complete his sixth novel, *Martin Chuzzlewit*. Early in his career, when he was struggling to become known, he signed a long-term contract with the publishers Chapman and Hall that was extremely beneficial for Chapman and Hall but much less so for Dickens himself. He felt as though he was working hard for little reward and had lost enthusiasm for the writing of *Martin Chuzzlewit*, which his reading public received coolly.

So the question is this: Should he fulfill his contractual obligations or should he risk a legal suit by temporarily abandoning the novel and publishing at his own expense a work closer to his heart, *A Christmas Carol*? The card on the left, **8 of Water—Stephen Blackpool**—represents the *Chuzzlewit* option, and the one on the right, **9 of Fire—Abel Magwitch**—the riskier possibility of striking out alone.

READING 1

8 of Water—Stephen Blackpool is a tragic figure. Trapped in a marriage with an alcoholic wife, he runs afoul of his coworkers when he refuses to engage in strike action. When the company boss solicits Stephen to spy on his union mates and he refuses, he is fired and forced to search for work elsewhere.

While traipsing across the countryside in search of employment, he falls into an open pit mine. He spends the remainder of the novel, *Hard Times*, immobilized on his back, staring up at the stars, before dying of his injuries. Back in his hometown, he has been framed for a bank robbery.

This card clearly indicates the abusive contract Dickens was saddled with, and had he persevered with the unpopular *Chuzzlewit*, the still-unproven author risked falling into disfavor with both his public and his financiers.

9 of Fire—Abel Magwitch is a renegade convict. He turns young Pip's world upside down, first by instilling in him an unsettling sense of conscience, then by bankrolling his education and subsequent worldly success. Magwitch himself works hard and becomes a financial success in Australia. He is a scapegoat, sacrificing his life to see his beloved Pip one last time at the conclusion of *Great Expectations*, which in turn compels Pip to see the error of his ways and change his life for the better.

This card suggests that the risk and sacrifice Dickens dared take in writing his special Christmas story would pay off in ways multiform and unforeseen. Like the ghosts that haunt Scrooge, Magwitch is something of a sorcerer; he reveals to us just what magic and resource man is able to conjure.

Magwitch escaped his indenture and, through a selfless act of generosity, redeemed himself and helped a child—just as Scrooge repents and helps Tiny Tim, and just as Dickens's bold about-face in producing *A Christmas Carol* has taught inestimable children the world over the blessings of kindness. One dark note that perhaps haunts this reading suggests that the writing of Christmas stories, which Dickens felt compelled to do every year after the mammoth success of *A Christmas Carol*, became for the author something of a prison.

READING 2

The second question concerns the nature of his relationship with his mistress, Ellen Ternan. The card on the left, **Father of Fire—Ralph Nickleby**, represents Charles Dickens; the card on the left, **Daughter of Earth—Florence Dombey**, represents Ellen Ternan; the central crowning card, **The Moon XVIII—The Mystery** (of Edwin Drood), represents the nature of the relationship itself.

Father of Fire—Ralph Nickleby is by all accounts a successful businessman. He offers to help his dead brother's destitute wife and children but develops an irrational hatred and jealousy of his nephew, Nicholas, and an unsavory and inappropriate interest in his pretty young niece, Kate. When he discovers that the simple-minded boy, Smike, whom Nicholas has befriended, is actually his own long-lost son, and that his cruel treatment of the boy has led to his death, Ralph is overcome with guilt and hangs himself. The implications here for Dickens

are that although he is a respected gentleman of wealth, prestige, and social standing, his actual concern for the Ternan family and his feelings for Ellen particularly were not as altruistic as he maintained. Ralph's jealousy of his vibrant nephew, Nicholas, suggests Dickens was perhaps attempting to regain some of his lost youth in his relations with Ellen, suffering as he was from a failed marriage, boredom, and the intimations of death, which are the hallmarks of a midlife crisis. The dead boy, Smike, may suggest Dickens's own children, whom he considered a disappointment, or the illegitimate baby boy Ellen bore Dickens but who died within his first year. The guilt Ralph is ravished with indicates the shame Dickens suffered from the secret affair, and this—along with the strain of keeping the affair hidden—may have directly contributed to his own early death.

Daughter of Earth—Florence Dombey is the compassionate, long-suffering daughter of the misogynistic businessman Paul Dombey. Here on the **Daughter of Earth** card, she is surrounded by two of the many men in her life who control her physical existence, but for whom she acts as anchor and heart. Florence is represented here by Dickens's own favorite daughter, Kate, who was as motivated and headstrong as he. As a court card, the **Daughter of Earth** signifies a strong filial bond—Ellen Ternan was Kate Dickens's own age, and the two women

remained on friendly terms long after Dickens's death.

There is some indication that Dickens's relationship with Ellen was that of a father to a daughter, and that Ellen was for him a beacon of tenderheartedness and emotional solace. After Dickens's death, like Flo Dombey, Ellen Ternan went on to marry and have two children, a boy and a girl.

The Moon XVIII—this card represents *The Mystery of Edwin Drood*, a novel about the secret passions of its central character, which Dickens left unfinished at his death. The male and female figures on the left are betrothed adolescents who decide not to marry, while their reflections on the right are orphaned siblings from the orient. The women are in nightclothes, as though sleepwalking; the men are dressed in respectable day attire. **The Moon** is the card of the subconscious, of unseen machinations and furtive desires. Dickens and Ternan's thirteen-year affair (13 being the number of moon phases in a year) had to be hidden from Victorian society, as under the veil of night. To be moonstruck is to be head over heels in love; to exhibit the effects of lunacy and mania is said to be manipulated by the moon. The ghostly church in the center of the card is Rochester Cathedral, in which Dickens was forbidden to wed Ternan but where he wished to be buried—a desire denied him, being interred in Poet's Corner instead. At the base of the card, an opium pipe rises like a puff adder toward a stained-glass full moon, known as a rose window. Together, these symbols represent the male and female aspects of humanity, the lingam and the yoni. The peace dove or Holy Ghost is the third aspect created out of this union, representing the wholeness of the union of opposites, the soul, the promise of life, or the spirit after death—said to travel from the earthly body to the Elysian Fields of the moon. As representative of the lovers' relationship, the card indicates that the male Dickens was emboldened and impassioned by the union, somewhat confused and conflicted, but also rejuvenated and revivified by Ellen Ternan's affection.

From Ellen's vantage, the relationship was one that compelled her to remain in the shadows, to act a role like a figure in a novel or a dream, to carry a torch but be denied being seen—especially from civil society and the religious sanction of the church. Years later, after Dickens's death, Ellen did reinvent herself, marry, and have two children—one male, one female—with her new husband, a clergyman.

The many narratives in the CDT lend themselves naturally to readings involving much-larger spreads that mimic novelistic forms such as the *Künstlerroman*, which focuses on the development of an artist's sensibility, or the bildungsroman, which—like the novel *David Copperfield*—follows an individual's development from youth to maturity. These spreads contain all the ingredients necessary for a discussion of self-actualization. Cards drawn for a reading that happen to originate from the same novel might be supposed to have particularly strong affinities. If a querent used **Son of Water—David Copperfield** as their signifier, for instance, any card drawn representing a character from *David Copperfield* inherently suggests deeper ties and more-diverse meanings in the overall fabric of the Tarot spread.

These cards include

4 of Fire—Betsey Trotwood;

Daughter of Fire—Dora Spenlow;

4 of Water—James Steerforth;

5 of Water—Rosa Dartle;

10 of Water—Yarmouth;

Mother of Water—Clara Peggotty;

7 of Air—Uriah Heep;

The Emperor IV—John Dickens.

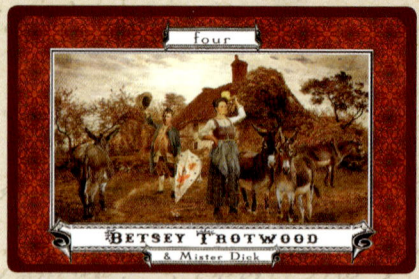

four

BETSEY TROTWOOD
& Mister Dick

ten

YARMOUTH

four

JAMES STEERFORTH

five

ROSA DARTLE

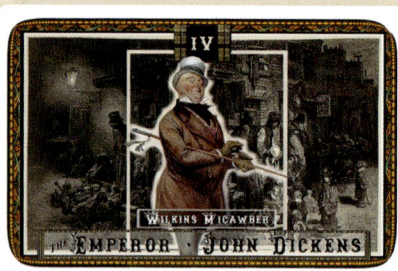

IV

WILKINS MICAWBER

THE EMPEROR · JOHN DICKENS

DAUGHTER

DORA SPENLOW

MOTHER

CLARA PEGGOTTY

seven

URIAH HEEP

NO THOROUGHFARE

A SUGGESTION OF SPREADS FOR THE CHARLES DICKENS TAROT

THE TALE OF TWO CITIES SPREAD
Number of cards: 1

As preparation for this spread, it is advised that the querent spend a few years binge drinking. When he or she has hit rock bottom, the reader pulls one card from the deck and places it in England. This card is "Charles Darnay" and represents everything the querent should be but isn't. Next, the Reader takes a Xerox or a Polaroid of the card and places it in France. If this proves difficult, the reader can quickly make a sketch of the card on a croissant. This is the "Sidney Carton" card and represents everything the querent was but no longer is and could be but isn't. With a standard household razor, slice the original "Charles Darnay" card in half. This may seem reactionary, reductionist, or even a little silly, but nevertheless it will find its way onto the public-school syllabus.

THE BARNABY RUDGE SPREAD
Number of cards: 78

Carefully shuffle the entire deck but put off the actual reading for five years. When you have the querent exactly where you want them, take all the cards and throw them at a Catholic. Calling yourself Grip and using clipped and cryptic speech, rearrange the scattered cards into the shape of a cross and set them on fire. The querent may wish to make arrangements with a taxidermist to have the reader stuffed.

THE BLEAK HOUSE SPREAD
Number of cards: 13

The querent carefully chooses twelve cards from a pile of a dozen cards the reader has already chosen. The querent then proceeds to construct from them a house of cards. Repeatedly asking the querent what his or her question is, the reader places the thirteenth card face down. This is the "Answer" card, which is to be revealed under no circumstances. Instead, soak the card in rum and mineral spirits and place it next to an open flame.

THE MARTIN CHUZZLEWIT SPREAD
Number of cards: fewer than expected

Take the cards and sort of move them around in a vague and unconvincing way. Have the querent choose a somewhat unlikable card, and send that card to Missouri. Other things happen in this spread, but the bit about Missouri is the only thing anyone will remember. If the reading is a success, the querent will contract malaria.

THE MYSTERY OF EDWIN DROOD SPREAD
Number of cards: that's a secret

This spread is best done late at night or when the reader is exhausted. Have the querent choose two cards—one from *The Charles Dickens Tarot* and one from *The Wilkie Collins Tarot*. The Reader should speak in a stereotypical East Indian accent and be moderately racist. Meanwhile, the querent should recline on their side. If there are any T3s in the house, now is the time to take them. If there are no T3s, cough syrup and a poppy seed bagel can be substituted. This is the halfway point of the reading, so stop and get on with your life.

THE *OLIVER!* SPREAD
Number of cards: 1

The Reader—ideally, an anti-Semite—gives the querent an empty bowl to hold. In it, the reader places a card face up. The reader says nothing. When the querent expresses curiosity, the reader knocks the bowl from the querent's hand and throws them out into the street. There, a song-and-dance routine takes place with lovable ragamuffins and, sadly, Davy Jones.

THE LITTLE NELL / OSCAR WILDE SPREAD
Number of cards: 1

The reader asks the querent to choose a card. The querent places the card face up on the table, and the reader proceeds to berate the querent in an exceedingly dry manner. This can go on all night, or as long as the absinthe lasts. With the querent at death's door, a memorable snide aside about the querent's long-awaited demise is made by the reader from Newgate Prison or a men's lavatory.

THE MR. PLORNISHMAROONTIGOONTER SPREAD
Number of cards: 10

The reader shuffles the deck and places a card face down on the table. The reader flips over the card, invents an idiosyncratic nickname for the card, and blames the querent for the many ways this card disappoints the reader. The reader goes on to do this once every year for the next ten years. The reader may choose to forbid some of the cards' marriages or disapprove of their career choices generally, but eventually the Reader *must* demand the cards discontinue all relations with their mother.

DICKENS'S CHRONOLOGICAL TIMELINE

1812 – On February 7, Charles Huffman Dickens is born in Portsmouth, the second child of John and Elizabeth Dickens.

1817–21 – The Dickens family moves to Chatham, outside Rochester. Charles, a sickly child, is educated by his mother and the books in his father's library. Dickens will later characterize these as the happiest years of his youth.

1822 – The Dickens family moves to London.

1824 – John Dickens arrested and sent to the Marshalsea prison. Charles Dickens begins work at the Warren's Blacking Factory two days after his 12th birthday. His memories of this time are traumatic and haunt much of his future work.

1825 – Charles schooled at Wellington House Academy.

1827 – Rejoins the workforce as a junior clerk at the legal firm of Ellis & Blackmore. Teaches himself shorthand and, by the end of 1828, leaves the law offices to become a chronicler of the affairs of Parliament.

1830 – Hired as a newspaper reporter for the *Mirror of Parliament*, a publication run by his uncle John Henry Burror. Dickens's father John is also employed here. Dickens meets Maria Beadnell, who becomes his first love.

1833 – Dickens's unrequited relationship with Maria Beadnell ends. Perhaps spurred on by romantic failure, Dickens' first story, "A Dinner at Poplar Walk," is published. He joins the prestigious *Morning Chronicle*. Here he writes his first sketches under the pseudonym Boz.

1834 – George Hogarth, editor of the *Evening Chronicle*, persuades Dickens to continue his Boz sketches for his paper. Becomes a regular guest at the Hogarth house where he meets George's daughters: Georgina, Mary, and his future wife Catherine.

1835 – Becomes engaged to Catherine, the eldest Hogarth daughter.

1836 – The day after Dickens's 24th birthday, his newspaper sketches are collected and published as Sketches by Boz and meet much acclaim. Ten days later, Dickens begins *The Pickwick Papers*. The day after April Fool's Day, Dickens marries Catherine Hogarth. In November, he becomes editor of *Bentley's Miscellany*. In December, Dickens meets his lifelong friend and future biographer, John Forster. *The Pickwick Papers* meantime catapult Dickens to instant fame.

1837 – Victoria ascends the throne. The first of Dickens's ten children, Charles Culliford Boz ("Flaster Floby," "theSnodgering Blee") Dickens, is born. Catherine begins to show the first signs of a lifelong neurosis. Mary Hogarth, of whom Dickens is inordinately fond, dies suddenly, aged 17. Dickens begins *OliverTwist*, which becomes immensely popular.

1838 – Dickens and Hablot Browne travel to Yorkshire to examine its boarding schools. Dickens's daughter Mary ("Mamie") is born. Dickens begins *Nicholas Nickleby*.

1839 – Dickens's daughter, KateMacready ("Lucifer Box"), is born.

1840 – Dickens begins the journal *Master Humphrey's Clock*, the content for which he is solely responsible. It begins running *The Old Curiosity Shop* in monthly installments. Dickens attends his first public hanging.

1841 – Dickens undertakes *Barnaby Rudge*, a novel he has been contemplating for some years. Charles and Catherine tour Scotland. Their son, Walter Savage Landor ("Young Skull"), is born. Dickens is asked to run for MP – he declines but nevertheless continues his public tirades against Tories, the child-labor laws, and factory conditions.

1842 – Charles and Catherine travel to America. Late in the year, Dickens begins work on *Martin Chuzzlewit*.

1843 – Dickens writes *A Christmas Carol*.

1844 – Dickens's son, Francis Jeffrey ("Chicken-Stalker"), is born. Dickens and family travel to Italy for eleven months. He treats Madame de la Rue with mesmerism.

1845 – Dickens's son, Alfred D'Orsay Tennyson ("Skittles"), is born. Directs and stars in Jonson's *Every Man In His Humour*.

1846 – Dickens's foray into newspaper journalism, *The Daily News*, folds within a month. The Dickens family spend half the year in Switzerland and the other half in Paris. Dickens begins *Dombey and Son*.

1847 – Miss Coutt's Home for Homeless Women opens. Dickens and his acting troupe, The Amateurs, put on *The Merry Wives of Windsor* for its benefit. Dickens's son, Sydney Smith Haldimand ("Ocean Spectre") is born.

1848 – Dickens's sister, Fanny, dies. *The Haunted Man*, his last Christmas book, is published.

1849 – Dickens's son, Henry Fielding ("Mr. H"), is born. Fanny's son, Henry Burnett, dies. Dickens begins *David Copperfield*.

1850 – Dickens's daughter, Dora Annie Dickens is born. *Household Words* is established with Dickens as editor and contributor.

1851 – Catherine Dickens suffers a nervous collapse. John Dickens dies. Dora Dickens dies, aged eight months. *What Shall We have for Dinner?*, a cookbook by Catherine Dickens, is published. Dickens performs in Bulwer Lytton's *Not As Bad As We Seem* before the queen. The Amateurs go on tour, during which Dickens strikes up a friendship with Wilkie Collins.

1852 – Dickens begins *Bleak House*. Hisson Edward Bulwer Lytton ("Mr.Plornishmaroontigoonter") Dickens, is born.

1853 – Dickens gives his first public reading in Birmingham—he designs this reading for working people and prices tickets accordingly.

1854 – Begins writing *Hard Times*.

1855 – Dickens has a disappointing reunion with his first love, Maria Winter née Beadnell. He begins writing *Little Dorrit*.

1856 – Dickens works with Wilkie Collins on *The Frozen Deep*. Purchases Gad's Hill Place.

1857 – Hans Christian Anderson is entertained at Gad's Hill. Dickens directs and stars in *The Frozen Deep*, co-authored by and co-starring Wilkie Collins. Queen Victoria sees it and is moved. The amateur cast, mostly made up of Dickens's family, is replaced by professional actors. Among them is Ellen Ternan whom Dickens falls madly in love with. His marriage strained, Dickens departs to Switzerland with Wilkie Collins and Augustus Egg for the remainder of the year.

1858 – Catherine Dickens confronts her husband about a bracelet intended for Ellen Ternan, which is mistakenly delivered to her. Dickens instructs her to meet with Nelly. Charles and Catherine separate, their children and Georgina Hogarth remaining with Dickens at Gad's Hill. To parry scandal, Dickens publishes a statement in the *Times* and *Household Words* denying accusations and justifying his actions. He embarks on his first major national reading tour, which numbers over 100 engagements. The response is tremendous, the results lucrative, but it ultimately contributes to his physical decline.

1859 – Begins *A Tale of Two Cities*. Undertakes another national reading tour. Starts a new journal entitled *All the Year Round*.

1860 – Begins writing *Great Expectations*. His daughter, Katie, a painter, marries painter Charles Perugini. Ten days later, his brother Alfred dies. Dickens burns his personal papers—a tradition he continues until his death.

1863 – Dickens's mother, Elizabeth, dies. Dickens's mother-in-law dies. Death of Dickens's son, Walter, in India. Death of William Makepeace Thackeray. Death of Augustus

1865 – Returning from France, Dickens is involved in the Staplehurst railway accident along with Ellen Ternan and her mother. Dickens keeps Nelly's name out of the papers; shows signs of suffering trauma. Finishes *Our Mutual Friend*.

1866 – Dickens moves Nelly and her mother to Slough.

1867 – Dickens settles Nelly permanently in Peckham. In November, he tours America for the second time.

1868 – Dickens cuts his American reading tour short. Back in England, he presents and perfects his *Murder of Nancy* reading. The result is a public success but irrevocably damages Dickens, both physically and psychologically.

1869 – Dickens is ordered by doctors to discontinue readings. Begins writing *The Mystery of Edwin Drood*.

1870 – Dickens delivers his farewell public reading to a London audience. On June 9, Charles Dickens collapses at Windsor Lodge, Nelly's residence in Peckham. Nelly takes the paralytic Dickens by closed coach to the waiting Georgina at Gad's Hill Place. His children are called. He dies later that day. Against his stated wishes, Dickens is not buried in Rochester but instead at Poet's Corner in Westminster Abbey.

CHRIS LEECH was born in Victoria, Canada.
He attended Catholic school and Victoria College of Art. He has lived
and worked in Germany, England, Greece, India, and Canada.
Chris is an artist (pierglass.wordpress.com) as well as a musician
and songwriter in the band Printers Bloc (printersbloc.org).
He is an avid book reader, gardener, and maker of Tarot decks
(shakespearetarot.com, beatlestarot.com,
goldenageofhollywoodtarot.com).